Singapore MATH

LEVEL 3

A&B

W9-CNP-802

Thinking Kids®
An imprint of Carson-Dellosa Publishing LLC
Greensboro, North Carolina

Copyright © 2015 Singapore Asia Publishers PTE LTD.

Thinking Kids®
An imprint of Carson-Dellosa Publishing LLC
PO Box 35665
Greensboro, NC 27425 USA

Printed in the USA • All rights reserved.   ISBN 978-1-4838-1320-2
09-137207784

Table of Contents

Table of Contents

INTRODUCTION TO SINGAPORE MATH

Welcome to Singapore Math! The math curriculum in Singapore has been recognized worldwide for its excellence in producing students highly skilled in mathematics. Students in Singapore have ranked at the top in the world in mathematics on the *Trends in International Mathematics and Science Study* (TIMSS) in 1993, 1995, 2003, and 2008. Because of this, Singapore Math has gained in interest and popularity in the United States.

Singapore Math curriculum aims to help students develop the necessary math concepts and process skills for everyday life and to provide students with the ability to formulate, apply, and solve problems. Mathematics in the Singapore Primary (Elementary) Curriculum cover fewer topics but in greater depth. Key math concepts are introduced and built on to reinforce various mathematical ideas and thinking. Students in Singapore are typically one grade level ahead of students in the United States.

The following pages provide examples of the various math problem types and skill sets taught in Singapore.

At an elementary level, some simple mathematical skills can help students understand mathematical principles. These skills are the counting-on, counting-back, and crossing-out methods. Note that these methods are most useful when the numbers are small.

1. The Counting-On Method

Used for addition of two numbers. Count on in 1s with the help of a picture or number line.

$$7 + 4 = 11$$

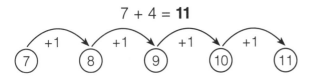

2. The Counting-Back Method

Used for subtraction of two numbers. Count back in 1s with the help of a picture or number line.

$$16 - 3 = 13$$

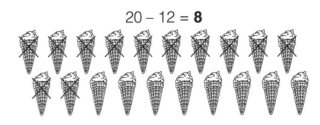

3. The Crossing-Out Method

Used for subtraction of two numbers. Cross out the number of items to be taken away. Count the remaining ones to find the answer.

$$20 - 12 = 8$$

A **number bond** shows the relationship in a simple addition or subtraction problem. The number bond is based on the concept "part-part-whole." This concept is useful in teaching simple addition and subtraction to young children.

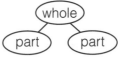

To find a whole, students must add the two parts.

To find a part, students must subtract the other part from the whole.

The different types of number bonds are illustrated on the next page.

1. Number Bond (single digits)

3 (part) + 6 (part) = **9** (whole)

9 (whole) − 3 (part) = **6** (part)

9 (whole) − 6 (part) = **3** (part)

2. Addition Number Bond (single digits)

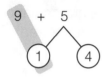

= 9 + 1 + 4   Make a ten first.

= 10 + 4

= **14**

3. Addition Number Bond (double and single digits)

= 2 + 5 + 10   Regroup 15 into 5 and 10.

= 7 + 10

= **17**

4. Subtraction Number Bond (double and single digits)

10 − 7 = 3

3 + 2 = **5**

5. Subtraction Number Bond (double digits)

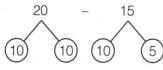

10 − 5 = 5

10 − 10 = 0

5 + 0 = **5**

Students should understand that multiplication is repeated addition and that division is the grouping of all items into equal sets.

1. Repeated Addition (Multiplication)

Mackenzie eats 2 rolls a day. How many rolls does she eat in 5 days?

$$2 + 2 + 2 + 2 + 2 = 10$$
$$5 \times 2 = 10$$

She eats **10** rolls in 5 days.

2. The Grouping Method (Division)

Mrs. Lee makes 14 sandwiches. She gives all the sandwiches equally to 7 friends. How many sandwiches does each friend receive?

$$14 \div 7 = 2$$

Each friend receives **2** sandwiches.

One of the basic but essential math skills students should acquire is to perform the 4 operations of whole numbers and fractions. Each of these methods is illustrated below.

1. The Adding-Without-Regrouping Method

```
  H  T  O          O: Ones
  3  2  1
+ 5  6  8          T: Tens
  ─────────
  8  8  9          H: Hundreds
```

Since no regrouping is required, add the digits in each place value accordingly.

2. The Adding-by-Regrouping Method

```
  H  T  O          O: Ones
 ¹4  9  2
+ 1  5  3          T: Tens
  ─────────
  6  4  5          H: Hundreds
```

In this example, regroup 14 tens into 1 hundred 4 tens.

Singapore Math Level 3A & 3B

3. The Adding-by-Regrouping-Twice Method

```
   H  T  O
  ¹2 ¹8  6
 +  3  6  5
 ───────────
   6  5  1
```

O: Ones
T: Tens
H: Hundreds

Regroup twice in this example.
First, regroup 11 ones into 1 ten 1 one.
Second, regroup 15 tens into 1 hundred 5 tens.

4. The Subtracting-Without-Regrouping Method

```
   H  T  O
   7  3  9
 -  3  2  5
 ───────────
   4  1  4
```

O: Ones
T: Tens
H: Hundreds

Since no regrouping is required, subtract the digits in each place value accordingly.

5. The Subtracting-by-Regrouping Method

```
   H   T   O
   5  ⁷8 ¹¹1
 -  2   4  7
 ─────────────
   3   3   4
```

O: Ones
T: Tens
H: Hundreds

In this example, students cannot subtract 7 ones from 1 one. So, regroup the tens and ones. Regroup 8 tens 1 one into 7 tens 11 ones.

6. The Subtracting-by-Regrouping-Twice Method

```
   H    T    O
  ⁷8  ⁹0  ¹⁰0
 -  5    9    3
 ───────────────
   2    0    7
```

O: Ones
T: Tens
H: Hundreds

In this example, students cannot subtract 3 ones from 0 ones and 9 tens from 0 tens. So, regroup the hundreds, tens, and ones. Regroup 8 hundreds into 7 hundreds 9 tens 10 ones.

7. The Multiplying-Without-Regrouping Method

```
   T  O
   2  4
 ×     2
 ────────
   4  8
```

O: Ones
T: Tens

Since no regrouping is required, multiply the digit in each place value by the multiplier accordingly.

8. The Multiplying-With-Regrouping Method

```
    H   T  O
   ¹3  ²4  9
 ×          3
 ────────────
  1, 0  4  7
```

O: Ones
T: Tens
H: Hundreds

In this example, regroup 27 ones into 2 tens 7 ones, and 14 tens into 1 hundred 4 tens.

9. The Dividing-Without-Regrouping Method

```
        2  4  1
     ┌─────────
   2 │ 4  8  2
      - 4
      ───
         8
       - 8
       ───
            2
          - 2
          ───
             0
```

Since no regrouping is required, divide the digit in each place value by the divisor accordingly.

10. The Dividing-With-Regrouping Method

```
        1  6  6
     ┌─────────
   5 │ 8  3  0
      - 5
      ───
         3  3
       - 3  0
       ──────
            3  0
          - 3  0
          ──────
               0
```

In this example, regroup 3 hundreds into 30 tens and add 3 tens to make 33 tens. Regroup 3 tens into 30 ones.

Singapore Math Level 3A & 3B

11. The Addition-of-Fractions Method

$$\frac{1}{6} \times \frac{2}{2} + \frac{1}{4} \times \frac{3}{3} = \frac{2}{12} + \frac{3}{12} = \frac{5}{12}$$

Always remember to make the denominators common before adding the fractions.

12. The Subtraction-of-Fractions Method

$$\frac{1}{2} \times \frac{5}{5} - \frac{1}{5} \times \frac{2}{2} = \frac{5}{10} - \frac{2}{10} = \frac{3}{10}$$

Always remember to make the denominators common before subtracting the fractions.

13. The Multiplication-of-Fractions Method

$$\frac{\overset{1}{\cancel{3}}}{5} \times \frac{1}{\underset{3}{\cancel{9}}} = \frac{1}{15}$$

When the numerator and the denominator have a common multiple, reduce them to their lowest fractions.

14. The Division-of-Fractions Method

$$\frac{7}{9} \div \frac{1}{6} = \frac{7}{\underset{3}{\cancel{9}}} \times \frac{\overset{2}{\cancel{6}}}{1} = \frac{14}{3} = 4\frac{2}{3}$$

When dividing fractions, first change the division sign ($\div$) to the multiplication sign ($\times$). Then, switch the numerator and denominator of the fraction on the right hand side. Multiply the fractions in the usual way.

Model drawing is an effective strategy used to solve math word problems. It is a visual representation of the information in word problems using bar units. By drawing the models, students will know of the variables given in the problem, the variables to find, and even the methods used to solve the problem.

Drawing models is also a versatile strategy. It can be applied to simple word problems involving addition, subtraction, multiplication, and division. It can also be applied to word problems related to fractions, decimals, percentage, and ratio.

The use of models also trains students to think in an algebraic manner, which uses symbols for representation.

The different types of bar models used to solve word problems are illustrated below.

1. The model that involves addition

Melissa has 50 blue beads and 20 red beads. How many beads does she have altogether?

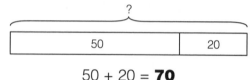

$$50 + 20 = \mathbf{70}$$

2. The model that involves subtraction

Ben and Andy have 90 toy cars. Andy has 60 toy cars. How many toy cars does Ben have?

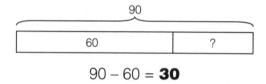

$$90 - 60 = \mathbf{30}$$

3. The model that involves comparison

Mr. Simons has 150 magazines and 110 books in his study. How many more magazines than books does he have?

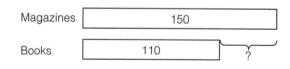

$$150 - 110 = \mathbf{40}$$

4. The model that involves two items with a difference

A pair of shoes costs $109. A leather bag costs $241 more than the pair of shoes. How much is the leather bag?

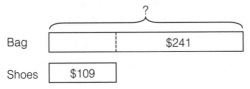

$$\$109 + \$241 = \textbf{\$350}$$

5. The model that involves multiples

Mrs. Drew buys 12 apples. She buys 3 times as many oranges as apples. She also buys 3 times as many cherries as oranges. How many pieces of fruit does she buy altogether?

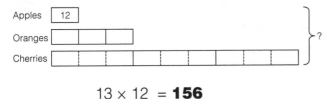

$$13 \times 12 = \textbf{156}$$

6. The model that involves multiples and difference

There are 15 students in Class A. There are 5 more students in Class B than in Class A. There are 3 times as many students in Class C than in Class A. How many students are there altogether in the three classes?

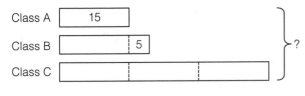

$$(5 \times 15) + 5 = \textbf{80}$$

7. The model that involves creating a whole

Ellen, Giselle, and Brenda bake 111 muffins. Giselle bakes twice as many muffins as Brenda. Ellen bakes 9 fewer muffins than Giselle. How many muffins does Ellen bake?

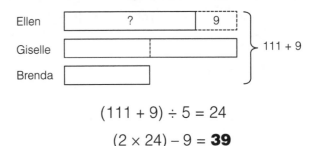

$$(111 + 9) \div 5 = 24$$
$$(2 \times 24) - 9 = \textbf{39}$$

8. The model that involves sharing

There are 183 tennis balls in Basket A and 97 tennis balls in Basket B. How many tennis balls must be transferred from Basket A to Basket B so that both baskets contain the same number of tennis balls?

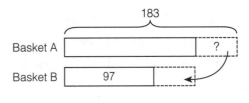

$$183 - 97 = 86$$
$$86 \div 2 = \textbf{43}$$

9. The model that involves fractions

George had 355 marbles. He lost $\frac{1}{5}$ of the marbles and gave $\frac{1}{4}$ of the remaining marbles to his brother. How many marbles did he have left?

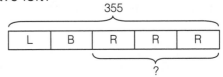

L: Lost
B: Brother
R: Remaining

$$5 \text{ parts} \rightarrow 355 \text{ marbles}$$
$$1 \text{ part} \rightarrow 355 \div 5 = 71 \text{ marbles}$$
$$3 \text{ parts} \rightarrow 3 \times 71 = \textbf{213} \text{ marbles}$$

10. The model that involves ratio

Aaron buys a tie and a belt. The prices of the tie and belt are in the ratio 2 : 5. If both items cost $539,

(a) what is the price of the tie?

(b) what is the price of the belt?

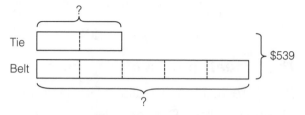

$539 ÷ 7 = $77

Tie (2 units) → 2 × $77 = **$154**

Belt (5 units) → 5 × $77 = **$385**

11. The model that involves comparison of fractions

Jack's height is $\frac{2}{3}$ of Leslie's height. Leslie's height is $\frac{3}{4}$ of Lindsay's height. If Lindsay is 160 cm tall, find Jack's height and Leslie's height.

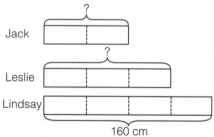

1 unit → 160 ÷ 4 = 40 cm

Leslie's height (3 units) → 3 × 40 = **120 cm**

Jack's height (2 units) → 2 × 40 = **80 cm**

Thinking skills and strategies are important in mathematical problem solving. These skills are applied when students think through the math problems to solve them. The following are some commonly used thinking skills and strategies applied in mathematical problem solving.

1. Comparing

Comparing is a form of thinking skill that students can apply to identify similarities and differences.

When comparing numbers, look carefully at each digit before deciding if a number is greater or less than the other. Students might also use a number line for comparison when there are more numbers.

Example:

3 is greater than 2 but smaller than 7.

2. Sequencing

A sequence shows the order of a series of numbers. *Sequencing* is a form of thinking skill that requires students to place numbers in a particular order. There are many terms in a sequence. The terms refer to the numbers in a sequence.

To place numbers in a correct order, students must first find a rule that generates the sequence. In a simple math sequence, students can either add or subtract to find the unknown terms in the sequence.

Example: Find the 7th term in the sequence below.

1,	4,	7,	10,	13,	16	?
1st term	2nd term	3rd term	4th term	5th term	6th term	7th term

Step 1: This sequence is in an increasing order.

Step 2: 4 – 1 = 3   7 – 4 = 3

The difference between two consecutive terms is 3.

Step 3: 16 + 3 = 19

The 7th term is **19**.

Singapore Math Level 3A & 3B

3. Visualization

Visualization is a problem solving strategy that can help students visualize a problem through the use of physical objects. Students will play a more active role in solving the problem by manipulating these objects.

The main advantage of using this strategy is the mobility of information in the process of solving the problem. When students make a wrong step in the process, they can retrace the step without erasing or canceling it.

The other advantage is that this strategy helps develop a better understanding of the problem or solution through visual objects or images. In this way, students will be better able to remember how to solve these types of problems.

Some of the commonly used objects for this strategy are toothpicks, straws, cards, strings, water, sand, pencils, paper, and dice.

4. Look for a Pattern

This strategy requires the use of observational and analytical skills. Students have to observe the given data to find a pattern in order to solve the problem. Math word problems that involve the use of this strategy usually have repeated numbers or patterns.

Example: Find the sum of all the numbers from 1 to 100.

Step 1: Simplify the problem.
Find the sum of 1, 2, 3, 4, 5, 6, 7, 8, 9, and 10.

Step 2: Look for a pattern.

$1 + 10 = 11$ $2 + 9 = 11$
$3 + 8 = 11$ $4 + 7 = 11$
$5 + 6 = 11$

Step 3: Describe the pattern.
When finding the sum of 1 to 10,

add the first and last numbers to get a result of 11. Then, add the second and second last numbers to get the same result. The pattern continues until all the numbers from 1 to 10 are added. There will be 5 pairs of such results. Since each addition equals 11, the answer is then $5 \times 11 = 55$.

Step 4: Use the pattern to find the answer.
Since there are 5 pairs in the sum of 1 to 10, there should be ($10 \times 5 = 50$ pairs) in the sum of 1 to 100.

Note that the addition for each pair is not equal to 11 now. The addition for each pair is now ($1 + 100 = 101$).

$50 \times 101 = 5050$

The sum of all the numbers from 1 to 100 is **5,050**.

5. Working Backward

The strategy of working backward applies only to a specific type of math word problem. These word problems state the end result, and students are required to find the total number. In order to solve these word problems, students have to work backward by thinking through the correct sequence of events. The strategy of working backward allows students to use their logical reasoning and sequencing to find the answers.

Example: Sarah has a piece of ribbon. She cuts the ribbon into 4 equal parts. Each part is then cut into 3 smaller equal parts. If the length of each small part is 35 cm, how long is the piece of ribbon?

$3 \times 35 = 105$ cm
$4 \times 105 = 420$ cm

The piece of ribbon is **420 cm**.

Singapore Math Level 3A & 3B

6. The Before-After Concept

The *Before-After* concept lists all the relevant data before and after an event. Students can then compare the differences and eventually solve the problems. Usually, the Before-After concept and the mathematical model go hand in hand to solve math word problems. Note that the Before-After concept can be applied only to a certain type of math word problem, which trains students to think sequentially.

Example: Kelly has 4 times as much money as Joey. After Kelly uses some money to buy a tennis racquet, and Joey uses $30 to buy a pair of pants, Kelly has twice as much money as Joey. If Joey has $98 in the beginning,

(a) how much money does Kelly have in the end?

(b) how much money does Kelly spend on the tennis racquet?

Before

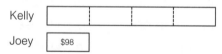

After

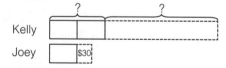

(a) $98 - $30 = $68

2 × $68 = $136

Kelly has **$136** in the end.

(b) 4 × $98 = $392

$392 − $136 = $256

Kelly spends **$256** on the tennis racquet.

7. Making Supposition

Making supposition is commonly known as "making an assumption." Students can use this strategy to solve certain types of math word problems. Making assumptions will eliminate some possibilities and simplifies the word problems by providing a boundary of values to work within.

Example: Mrs. Jackson bought 100 pieces of candy for all the students in her class. How many pieces of candy would each student receive if there were 25 students in her class?

In the above word problem, assume that each student received the same number of pieces. This eliminates the possibilities that some students would receive more than others due to good behavior, better results, or any other reason.

8. Representation of Problem

In problem solving, students often use representations in the solutions to show their understanding of the problems. Using representations also allow students to understand the mathematical concepts and relationships as well as to manipulate the information presented in the problems. Examples of representations are diagrams and lists or tables.

Diagrams allow students to consolidate or organize the information given in the problems. By drawing a diagram, students can see the problem clearly and solve it effectively.

A list or table can help students organize information that is useful for analysis. After analyzing, students can then see a pattern, which can be used to solve the problem.

9. Guess and Check

One of the most important and effective problem-solving techniques is *Guess and Check*. It is also known as *Trial and Error*. As the name suggests, students have to guess the answer to a problem and check if that guess is correct. If the guess is wrong, students will make another guess. This will continue until the guess is correct.

It is beneficial to keep a record of all the guesses and checks in a table. In addition, a *Comments* column can be included. This will enable students to analyze their guess (if it is too high or too low) and improve on the next guess. Be careful; this problem-solving technique can be tiresome without systematic or logical guesses.

Example: Jessica had 15 coins. Some of them were 10-cent coins and the rest were 5-cent coins. The total amount added up to $1.25. How many coins of each kind were there?

Use the guess-and-check method.

Number of 10¢ Coins	Value	Number of 5¢ Coins	Value	Total Number of Coins	Total Value
7	$7 \times 10¢ = 70¢$	8	$8 \times 5¢ = 40¢$	$7 + 8 = 15$	$70¢ + 40¢ = 110¢$ $= \$1.10$
8	$8 \times 10¢ = 80¢$	7	$7 \times 5¢ = 35¢$	$8 + 7 = 15$	$80¢ + 35¢ = 115¢$ $= \$1.15$
10	$10 \times 10¢ = 100¢$	5	$5 \times 5¢ = 25¢$	$10 + 5 = 15$	$100¢ + 25¢ = 125¢$ $= \$1.25$

There were **ten** 10-cent coins and **five** 5-cent coins.

10. Restate the Problem

When solving challenging math problems, conventional methods may not be workable. Instead, restating the problem will enable students to see some challenging problems in a different light so that they can better understand them.

The strategy of restating the problem is to "say" the problem in a different and clearer way. However, students have to ensure that the main idea of the problem is not altered.

How do students restate a math problem?

First, read and understand the problem. Gather the given facts and unknowns. Note any condition(s) that have to be satisfied.

Next, restate the problem. Imagine narrating this problem to a friend. Present the given facts, unknown(s), and condition(s). Students may want to write the "revised" problem. Once the "revised" problem is analyzed, students should be able to think of an appropriate strategy to solve it.

11. Simplify the Problem

One of the commonly used strategies in mathematical problem solving is simplification of the problem. When a problem is simplified, it can be "broken down" into two or more smaller parts. Students can then solve the parts systematically to get to the final answer.

13

3A LEARNING OUTCOMES

Unit 1 Numbers 1–10,000
Students should be able to
- recognize and write numbers up to 10,000 in numerals and words.
- understand the place value of numbers up to 10,000.
- compare and arrange numbers up to 10,000.
- complete number patterns.

Unit 2 Adding Numbers up to 10,000
Students should be able to
- add numbers up to 10,000.
- perform addition by regrouping ones, tens, and hundreds.
- solve up to 2-step addition word problems.

Review 1
This review tests students' understanding of Units 1 & 2.

Unit 3 Subtracting Numbers up to 10,000
Students should be able to
- subtract numbers up to 10,000.
- perform subtraction by regrouping ones, tens, hundreds, and thousands.
- solve up to 2-step subtraction word problems.

Unit 4 Problem Solving (Adding and Subtracting)
Students should be able to
- solve up to 2-step word problems related to addition and subtraction.

Review 2
This review tests students' understanding of Units 3 & 4.

Unit 5 Multiplying Numbers by 6, 7, 8, and 9
Students should be able to
- multiply numbers by 6, 7, 8, and 9.
- divide numbers by 6, 7, 8, and 9.
- solve up to 2-step multiplication word problems.

Unit 6 Multiplying Numbers
Students should be able to
- multiply numbers without regrouping.
- multiply numbers by regrouping ones, tens, hundreds, and thousands.
- solve up to 2-step multiplication word problems.

Review 3
This review tests students' understanding of Units 5 & 6.

Unit 7 Dividing Numbers
Students should be able to
- divide numbers by regrouping hundreds, tens, and ones.
- find quotients and remainders by dividing.
- identify odd and even numbers.
- solve up to 2-step division word problems.

Unit 8 Problem Solving (Multiplying and Dividing)
Students should be able to
- solve up to 2-step word problems involving addition, subtraction, multiplication, and division.

Unit 9 Mental Calculations
Students should be able to
- mentally add and subtract two 2-digit numbers.
- mentally multiply and divide numbers within the multiplication table up to 10×10.

Review 4
This review tests students' understanding of Units 7, 8, & 9.

Mid-Review
This review is an excellent assessment of students' understanding of all the topics in the first half of this book.

Singapore Math Level 3A & 3B

FORMULA SHEET

Unit 1 Numbers 1–10,000
4-digit numbers can be written in numerals or words.
Example: Write 8,945 in words.
eight thousand, nine hundred forty-five

Place value
In a 4-digit number, each digit has a different value. The place value is used to identify the particular place of a digit, such as thousands, hundreds, tens, or ones, and its value.

Example:
In 3,785,
the digit 3 is in the **thousands** place.
the digit 3 stands for **3,000**.
the value of the digit 3 is **3,000**.

Comparing numbers
Begin by comparing the 2 numbers from the thousands place.
- When one number is bigger than the other, use the words *greater than* to describe it.
- When one number is smaller than the other, use the words *smaller than* to describe it.

Order and Pattern
When arranging a set of numbers in order,
- determine if the series must begin with the largest or the smallest number,
- compare the place value of the numbers,
- arrange the numbers in the correct order.

For number pattern problems,
- determine if the number pattern is in an increasing or a decreasing order,
- find the difference between 2 consecutive numbers,
- apply the difference to find the unknown number.

More than and Less than
Replace the words *more than* with an addition sign (+).
Example: What is 1,000 more than 6,007?
1,000 + 6,007 = 7,007

Replace the words *less than* with a subtraction sign (–).
Example: What is 1,000 less than 6,007?
      6,007 – 1,000 = 5,007

Unit 2 Adding Numbers up to 10,000
The word *sum* means addition.
Adding without regrouping
- Add the digits in the ones place first.
- Add the digits in the tens place.
- Add the digits in the hundreds place.
- Add the digits in the thousands place.

Adding with regrouping
- Add the digits in the ones place first. Regroup the ones if there are more than 10 ones.
- Add the digits in the tens place. Add another ten if there is a regrouping of ones. Regroup the tens if there are more than 10 tens.
- Add the digits in the hundreds place. Add another hundred if there is a regrouping of tens. Regroup the hundreds if there are more than 10 hundreds.
- Add the digits in the thousands place. Add another thousand if there is a regrouping of hundreds.

Unit 3 Subtracting Numbers up to 10,000
The word *difference* means subtraction.
Subtracting without regrouping
- Subtract the digits in the ones place first.
- Subtract the digits in the tens place.
- Subtract the digits in the hundreds place.
- Subtract the digits in the thousands place.

Subtracting with regrouping
- Subtract the digits in the ones place first. If this is not possible, regroup the tens and ones.
- Subtract the digits in the tens place. If this is not possible, regroup the hundreds and tens.
- Subtract the digits in the hundreds place. Regroup the thousands and hundreds if needed.
- Subtract the digits in the thousands place.

Unit 4 Problem Solving (Adding and Subtracting)
Below are suggested steps for solving addition and subtraction problems.

1. First, read and understand the problem.
2. Look for keywords to determine whether to add or subtract.
3. Draw models to help you understand the problem better.
4. Write the number sentences.
5. Remember to write your answers in the number sentences.
6. Write a statement to answer the word problem. You can underline the final answer in the statement.

Unit 5 Multiplying Numbers by 6, 7, 8, and 9
Below are the multiplication tables for 6, 7, 8, and 9.

×	6	7	8	9
1	6	7	8	9
2	12	14	16	18
3	18	21	24	27
4	24	28	32	36
5	30	35	40	45
6	36	42	48	54
7	42	49	56	63
8	48	56	64	72
9	54	63	72	81
10	60	70	80	90
11	66	77	88	99
12	72	84	96	108

Singapore Math Level 3A & 3B

Unit 6 Multiplying Numbers

The terms in multiplication are:

multiplicand × multiplier = product

Multiplying without regrouping
- Multiply the digit in the ones place by the multiplier first.
- Multiply the digit in the tens place by the multiplier.
- Multiply the digit in the hundreds place by the multiplier.

Multiplying with regrouping
- Multiply the digit in the ones place by the multiplier first. Regroup the ones if there are more than 10 ones.
- Multiply the digit in the tens place by the multiplier. Remember to add the tens from the regrouping of ones if there are any. Regroup the tens if there are more than 10 tens.
- Multiply the digit in the hundreds place by the multiplier. Remember to add the hundreds from the regrouping of tens if there are any. Regroup the hundreds if there are more than 10 hundreds.

Unit 7 Dividing Numbers

The terms in division are:

dividend ÷ divisor = quotient and remainder

When the dividend can be divided equally by the divisor, there will be no remainder.

When the dividend cannot be divided equally by the divisor, there will be a remainder. The remainder will be less than the divisor.

Knowing the multiplication tables make division faster and easier.

Division without regrouping
- Divide the digit in the hundreds place by the divisor first.
- Divide the digit in the tens place by the divisor.
- Divide the digit in the ones place by the divisor.

Division with regrouping
- Divide the digit in the hundreds place by the divisor first. Find the remainder of hundreds if there is any.
- Regroup the remainder of hundreds to tens. Add up all tens. Divide the tens by the divisor. Find the remainder of tens if there is any.
- Regroup the remainder of tens to ones. Add up all ones. Divide the ones by the divisor. Find the remainder if there is any.

Odd numbers are numbers that will have a remainder of 1 when divided by 2.
Examples of odd numbers: 1, 3, 5, 7, 9, 11, ...

Even numbers are numbers that will have no remainder when divided by 2.
Examples of even numbers: 2, 4, 6, 8, 10, 12, ...

Unit 8 Problem Solving (Multiplying and Dividing)

Below are suggested steps for solving multiplication and division problems.

1. First, read and understand the problem.
2. Look for keywords to determine whether to multiply or divide.
3. Draw models to help you understand the problem better.
4. Write the number sentences.
5. Remember to write your answers in the number sentences.
6. Write a statement to answer the word problem. You can underline the final answer in the statement.

Unit 9 Mental Calculations

Adding mentally

Method 1

Step 1: Break up one of the addends into tens and ones.

Step 2: Add the other addend to the tens in Step 1.

Step 3: Add the remaining ones to the result in Step 2.

Method 2

Step 1: Round one of the addends to the nearest ten. Remember to find the difference between the addend and the rounded number.

Step 2: Add the rounded number to the other addend.

Step 3: Subtract the difference in Step 1 from the result obtained in Step 2.

Method 3

Step 1: Round one of the addends to 100. Remember to find the difference between the addend and 100.

Step 2: Add 100 to the other addend.

Step 3: Subtract the difference in Step 1 from the result obtained in Step 2.

Subtracting mentally

Method 1

Step 1: Break up one of the subtrahends into tens and ones.

Step 2: Subtract the tens in Step 1 from the other subtrahend.

Step 3: Subtract the remaining ones from the result obtained in Step 2.

Method 2

Step 1: Round one of the subtrahends to the nearest ten. Remember to find the difference between the subtrahend and the rounded number.

Step 2: Subtract the rounded number from the other subtrahend.

Step 3: Add the difference in Step 1 to the result obtained in Step 2.

Multiplying and Dividing mentally

In order to multiply and divide quickly and accurately, you must memorize the multiplication tables from 2 to 10.

When multiplying and dividing tens or hundreds by a number, substitute the zeros in the tens and hundreds the words *tens* or *hundreds*. This makes the numbers smaller and more manageable.

Singapore Math Level 3A & 3B

Unit 1: NUMBERS 1–10,000

Examples:

1. Write 3,208 in words.   <u>three thousand, two hundred eight</u>

2. In 6,927,
   (a) the digit **2** is in the tens place.
   (b) the digit 9 is in the **hundreds** place.
   (c) the value of the digit **7** is 7.
   (d) the value of the digit 6 is **6,000**.
   (e) the digit 9 stands for **900**.

3. Arrange these numbers in order. Begin with the smallest.

   4,205, 3,761, 4,502, 6,389   <u>**3,761, 4,205, 4,502, 6,389**</u>

4. Complete the number pattern below.

   1,936, **2,036**, **2,136**, 2,236, 2,336, **2,436**

Write the numbers on the lines.

1. three thousand, six hundred twenty-five   _3,625_

2. nine thousand, ninety-nine   _9,099_

3. six thousand, two hundred eight   _6,208_

4. five thousand, eight hundred seventeen   _5,817_

5. eight thousand, thirty-five   _8,035_

Singapore Math Level 3A & 3B

Write the following numbers as words on the lines.

6. 9,693 _ninethousand_

7. 4,313 _____

8. 8,440 _____

9. 7,015 _____

10. 6,505 _____

Count the numbers by tens, hundreds, or thousands. Write the correct answer in each blank.

11. (8,050) (8,060) (   ) (8,080) (   )

12. (2,111) (   ) (2,311) (   ) (2,511)

13. (3,593) (4,593) (   ) (6,593) (   )

14. (1,999) (   ) (2,199) (2,299) (   )

15. (7,080) (   ) (7,100) (   ) (7,120)

Fill in each blank with the correct answer.

16. 3,740 = _____ thousands _____ hundreds _____ tens _____ ones

17. 9,361 = _____ thousands _____ hundreds _____ tens _____ one

18. 7,001 = _____ thousands _____ hundreds _____ tens _____ one

19. 6,384 = _____ + _____ + _____ + _____

20. 1,072 = _____ + _____ + _____ + _____

Singapore Math Level 3A & 3B

21. $4,951 =$ _____ + _____ + _____ + _____

22. $5,818 = 5,000 +$ _____ $+ 10 + 8$

23. $2,756 =$ _____ $+ 700 + 50 + 6$

24. $8,668 = 8,000 +$ _____ $+ 60 + 8$

25. In 1,540,

    (a)   the digit _____ is in the ones place.

    (b)   the digit 1 is in the _____ place.

    (c)   the value of the digit 5 is _____.

    (d)   the value of the digit _____ is 40.

26. In 8,429,

    (a)   the digit _____ is in the hundreds place.

    (b)   the digit 9 is in the _____ place.

    (c)   the value of the digit 2 is _____.

    (d)   the value of the digit _____ is 8,000.

27. In 5,741,

    (a)   the digit _____ is in the thousands place.

    (b)   the digit 4 is in the _____ place.

    (c)   the value of the digit 7 is _____.

    (d)   the value of the digit _____ is 1.

Singapore Math Level 3A & 3B

Circle the smaller number in each pair.

28.   6,447   6,474

29.   1,704   1,047

30.   4,196   8,196

Circle the larger number in each pair.

31.   6,456   6,656

32.   8,294   8,942

33.   3,010   3,001

Circle the largest number in each set.

34.   4,614   4,216   4,461

35.   9,909   9,999   9,099

36.   5,115   5,515   5,551

Circle the smallest number in each set.

37.   8,624   2,468   2,648

38.   3,829   3,920   9,833

39.   5,625   6,250   2,056

Fill in each blank with *greater* **or** *smaller.*

40. 1,068 is _____ than 1,168.

41. 8,843 is _____ than 8,803.

42. 7,452 is _____ than 5,252.

43. 3,090 is _____ than 309.

44. 4,234 is _____ than 4,324.

Complete the number patterns.

45. 1,540, 1,545, _____, _____, 1,560

46. 4,869, _____, 4,669, 4,569, _____

47. 2,330, 2,340, _____, 2,360, _____

48. 8,719, _____, _____, 5,719, 4,719

49. 5,876, 5,886, _____, _____, 5,916

Arrange the following numbers in order. Begin with the largest.

50. | 3,619 | | 6,193 | | 1,936 | | 9,316 |

_____, _____, _____, _____

51. | 5,805 | | 5,508 | | 5,850 | | 5,058 |

_____, _____, _____, _____

Singapore Math Level 3A & 3B

52. | 9,396 | | 6,939 | | 3,699 | | 9,963 |

_____, _____, _____, _____

53. | 4,120 | | 2,014 | | 4,210 | | 2,104 |

_____, _____, _____, _____

54. | 6,818 | | 6,881 | | 8,116 | | 8,616 |

_____, _____, _____, _____

Arrange the following numbers in order. Begin with the smallest.

55. | 2,424 | | 8,424 | | 4,424 | | 1,424 |

_____, _____, _____, _____

56. | 8,011 | | 8,101 | | 8,001 | | 8,118 |

_____, _____, _____, _____

57. | 5,240 | | 4,025 | | 5,045 | | 4,520 |

_____, _____, _____, _____

58. | 6,339 | | 6,933 | | 3,693 | | 3,369 |

_____, _____, _____, _____

59. | 4,916 | | 4,169 | | 4,691 | | 4,619 |

_____,   _____,   _____,   _____

60. What is the largest 4-digit number you can make using the digits 6, 2, 8, and 1?

_____

61. What is the smallest 4-digit number you can make using the digits 9, 3, 5, and 7?

_____

Unit 2: ADDING NUMBERS UP TO 10,000

Examples:

1. Find the sum of 5,420 and 3,519.

$$\begin{array}{r} 5,4\ 2\ 0 \\ +\ 3,5\ 1\ 9 \\ \hline 8,9\ 3\ 9 \end{array}$$

2. Find the sum of 2,847 and 4,753.

$$\begin{array}{r} {}^{1}\ {}^{1}\ {}^{1}\quad \\ 2,8\ 4\ 7 \\ +\ 4,7\ 5\ 3 \\ \hline 7,6\ 0\ 0 \end{array}$$

Find the sum of the following numbers.

1.   1,386 and 2,001 = _____

2.   5,210 and 4,689 = _____

3.   4,037 and 2,232 = _____

4.   6,512 and 3,076 = _____

5.   4,378 and 1,521 = _____

Fill in each blank with the correct answer.

6.   3 hundreds 6 tens + 8 hundreds 3 tens

= ____ hundreds ____ tens

= ____ thousand ____ hundred ____ tens

Singapore Math Level 3A & 3B

7. 5 hundreds 9 tens 3 ones + 6 hundreds 4 tens 2 ones

= ____ hundreds ____ tens ____ ones

= ____ thousand ____ hundreds ____ tens ____ ones

8. 7 hundreds 6 tens 9 ones + 5 hundreds 2 tens 4 ones

= ____ hundreds ____ tens ____ ones

= ____ thousand ____ hundreds ____ tens ____ ones

9. 4 hundreds 2 tens 5 ones + 8 hundreds 8 tens 9 ones

= ____ hundreds ____ tens ____ ones

= ____ thousand ____ hundreds ____ ten ____ ones

10. 9 hundreds 1 ten 5 ones + 8 hundreds 5 tens

= ____ hundreds ____ tens ____ ones

= ____ thousand ____ hundreds ____ tens ____ ones

Fill in each blank with the correct answer.

11. The sum of 2,790 and 5,637 is _____.

12. The sum of 4,078 and 3,659 is _____.

13. The sum of 8,316 and 1,473 is _____.

Singapore Math Level 3A & 3B

Add the following numbers. Show your work.

14.
$$
\begin{array}{r}
1{,}745 \\
+\ 6{,}487 \\
\hline
\end{array}
$$

19.
$$
\begin{array}{r}
2{,}282 \\
+\ 5{,}413 \\
\hline
\end{array}
$$

15.
$$
\begin{array}{r}
8{,}400 \\
+\ 1{,}324 \\
\hline
\end{array}
$$

20.
$$
\begin{array}{r}
4{,}908 \\
+\ 1{,}767 \\
\hline
\end{array}
$$

16.
$$
\begin{array}{r}
3{,}356 \\
+\ 4{,}134 \\
\hline
\end{array}
$$

21.
$$
\begin{array}{r}
6{,}210 \\
+\ 1{,}538 \\
\hline
\end{array}
$$

17.
$$
\begin{array}{r}
4{,}348 \\
+\ 1{,}625 \\
\hline
\end{array}
$$

22.
$$
\begin{array}{r}
9{,}126 \\
+\ \ \ \ 142 \\
\hline
\end{array}
$$

18.
$$
\begin{array}{r}
7{,}430 \\
+\ 1{,}932 \\
\hline
\end{array}
$$

23.
$$
\begin{array}{r}
4{,}813 \\
+\ 4{,}135 \\
\hline
\end{array}
$$

Singapore Math Level 3A & 3B

24.　　5,4 1 0
　　　+ 2,3 8 5
　　　—————

29.　　6,2 8 1
　　　+ 1,1 9 8
　　　—————

25.　　3,8 6 9
　　　+ 2,4 3 5
　　　—————

30.　　4,6 3 3
　　　+ 3,0 4 7
　　　—————

26.　　3,8 6 3
　　　+ 5,5 7 6
　　　—————

31.　　2,2 8 2
　　　+ 4,0 6 0
　　　—————

27.　　5,6 5 7
　　　+ 3,6 3 8
　　　—————

32.　　3,6 3 2
　　　+ 6,2 6 1
　　　—————

28.　　5,3 7 5
　　　+ 2,9 1 7
　　　—————

Match each butterfly to the correct flower.

33.  4,147 + 2,836

 • 6,144

34.  1,939 + 4,205

 • 3,527

35. 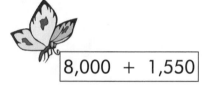 8,000 + 1,550

 • 9,550

36. 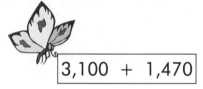 3,100 + 1,470

 • 4,570

37.  2,020 + 1,507

• 6,983

Singapore Math Level 3A & 3B

Solve the following word problems. Show your work in the space below.

38. Shop A sells 3,279 cans of drinks. Shop B sells 2,580 cans of drinks. How many cans of drinks do both shops sell altogether?

39. Sam spent $1,574 in January. He spent $3,100 in February. How much did he spend altogether?

40. Jerry, a truck driver, traveled 4,200 km in June. He traveled 1,935 km more in July. How far did he travel in July?

41. Ben collects 4,164 bottle caps. William collects 2,659 bottle caps more than Ben. How many bottle caps does William collect?

42. Tomás sold 2,347 pens in February. He sold 3,169 pens in March. How many pens did he sell in the 2 months?

REVIEW 1

Write the following numbers as words on the lines.

1. 1,915 _____

2. 6,306 _____

Write the numbers on the lines.

3. three thousand, twelve   _____

4. eight thousand, two hundred twenty-eight   _____

Add the following numbers. Show your work.

5.   4,3 7 9
    + 2,4 6 8
    _____

7.   5,3 8 5
    + 2,4 1 8
    _____

6.   1,0 0 2
    + 2,8 9 9
    _____

8.   4,0 1 6
    + 3,8 4 9
    _____

Circle the smaller number in each pair.

9. 4,879   4,798

10. 1,050   1,500

Circle the largest number in each set.

11. 3,711   3,177   3,717

12. 6,023   6,203   6,032

Complete the number patterns.

13. 4,614, 4,624, _____, _____, 4,654

14. 7,899, _____, 7,937, 7,956, _____

Arrange the following numbers in order. Begin with the smallest.

15. | 4,860 | | 6,048 | | 4,680 | | 6,840 |

_____,   _____,   _____,   _____

Fill in each blank with the correct answer.

16. In 2,036,

(a) the digit _____ is in the thousands place.

(b) the value of the digit 6 is _____.

(c) the digit 0 is in the _____ place.

(d) the value of the digit _____ is 30.

Singapore Math Level 3A & 3B

17. The sum of 7,096 and 1,845 is _____.

18. 4 hundreds 3 tens 4 ones + 9 hundreds 1 ten 5 ones

    = _____ hundreds _____ tens _____ ones

    = _____ thousand _____ hundreds _____ tens _____ ones

Solve the following word problems. Show your work in the space below.

19. Kwame saved $4,312 in March. He saved $688 more in April than in March. How much did he save in April?

20. Mandy pays $1,375 for a diamond bracelet. She pays $1,999 more for a diamond necklace. How much does Mandy pay for the diamond necklace?

Singapore Math Level 3A & 3B

Unit 3: SUBTRACTING NUMBERS UP TO 10,000

Examples:

1. Find the difference between 6,283 and 4,041.

$$\begin{array}{r} 6,283 \\ -\ 4,041 \\ \hline 2,242 \end{array}$$

2. Find the difference between 9,000 and 3,645.

$$\begin{array}{r} \overset{8\ \ 9\ \ 9\ \ 10}{9,000} \\ -\ 3,645 \\ \hline 5,355 \end{array}$$

Find the difference between the following numbers.

1. 67 and 17 = _____

2. 53 and 12 = _____

3. 548 and 320 = _____

4. 486 and 35 = _____

5. 979 and 546 = _____

Singapore Math Level 3A & 3B

Solve the following subtraction problems. Show your work.

6.
$$
\begin{array}{r}
3,869 \\
-\quad 235 \\
\hline
\end{array}
$$

12.
$$
\begin{array}{r}
6,848 \\
-\ 2,005 \\
\hline
\end{array}
$$

7.
$$
\begin{array}{r}
7,787 \\
-\ 4,325 \\
\hline
\end{array}
$$

13.
$$
\begin{array}{r}
2,426 \\
-\ 1,310 \\
\hline
\end{array}
$$

8.
$$
\begin{array}{r}
9,776 \\
-\ 1,085 \\
\hline
\end{array}
$$

14.
$$
\begin{array}{r}
7,431 \\
-\ 5,611 \\
\hline
\end{array}
$$

9.
$$
\begin{array}{r}
5,881 \\
-\ 4,058 \\
\hline
\end{array}
$$

15.
$$
\begin{array}{r}
8,818 \\
-\ 7,107 \\
\hline
\end{array}
$$

10.
$$
\begin{array}{r}
2,900 \\
-\quad 890 \\
\hline
\end{array}
$$

16.
$$
\begin{array}{r}
9,130 \\
-\ 3,684 \\
\hline
\end{array}
$$

11.
$$
\begin{array}{r}
4,136 \\
-\ 2,128 \\
\hline
\end{array}
$$

17.
$$
\begin{array}{r}
8,292 \\
-\ 2,505 \\
\hline
\end{array}
$$

Singapore Math Level 3A & 3B

18.
$$5,392$$
$$-\ 2,886$$

22.
$$8,000$$
$$-\ 4,659$$

19.
$$4,988$$
$$-\ 3,969$$

23.
$$3,576$$
$$-\ 1,899$$

20.
$$9,368$$
$$-\ 1,487$$

24.
$$6,005$$
$$-\ 4,769$$

21.
$$2,376$$
$$-\ 1,487$$

25.
$$8,010$$
$$-\ 3,865$$

Fill in each blank with the correct answer.

26. $4,369 - 3,124 = $ _____

27. $5,139 - 2,000 = $ _____

28. $5,353 - 1,526 = $ _____

29. $3,350 - 1,598 = $ _____

30. $6,206 - 2,062 = $ _____

Singapore Math Level 3A & 3B

31. Cameron is expecting a gift from his father. Solve the subtraction problems, and write the correct letter in each box to reveal the gift Cameron gets from his father.

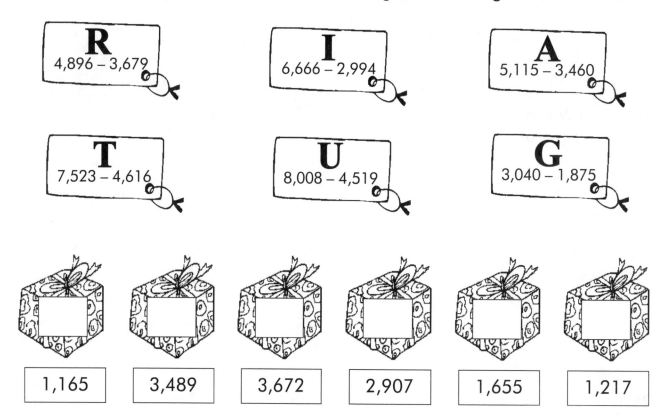

R
4,896 – 3,679

I
6,666 – 2,994

A
5,115 – 3,460

T
7,523 – 4,616

U
8,008 – 4,519

G
3,040 – 1,875

| 1,165 | 3,489 | 3,672 | 2,907 | 1,655 | 1,217 |

Solve the following word problems. Show your work in the space below.

32. Hafiz has 4,376 stickers in his collection. Alex has 2,950 fewer stickers. How many stickers does Alex have?

Singapore Math Level 3A & 3B

33. Amelia uses 2,315 beads to make a necklace. She uses 1,670 beads to make a bracelet. How many fewer beads does she use for the bracelet?

34. Alicia baked 5,300 muffins in June. She baked 565 fewer muffins in July. How many muffins did Alicia bake in July?

35. LaTonya pays $6,478 for a television set. She pays $2,590 less for a laptop. How much does the laptop cost?

36. Rosa sold some stamps on Monday. She sold 4,825 stamps on Tuesday. The total number of stamps she sold on these 2 days was 9,000. How many stamps did she sell on Monday?

Singapore Math Level 3A & 3B

Unit 4: PROBLEM SOLVING (ADDING AND SUBTRACTING)

Examples:

1. Jessie bought a purse for $999. She bought a dress for $199. How much did she spend altogether?

Solution:

The keyword *altogether* suggests that we should add the 2 numbers.

$999	$199

?

$$\begin{array}{r} \overset{1\ \ 1}{9}\ 9\ 9 \\ +\ \ 1\ 9\ 9 \\ \hline 1,1\ 9\ 8 \end{array}$$

$999 + $199 = $1,198

She spent **$1,198** altogether.

2. Aunt Grace baked 1,200 pineapple tarts last week. She baked 1,855 pineapple tarts this week. How many more pineapple tarts did she bake this week?

Solution:

The keyword *more* usually suggests addition. However, it means subtraction here, as we want to find out how many more pineapple tarts Aunt Grace baked this week.

This week	1,855
Last week	1,200	?

$$\begin{array}{r} 1,8\ 5\ 5 \\ -\ 1,2\ 0\ 0 \\ \hline 6\ 5\ 5 \end{array}$$

1855 – 1200 = 655

She baked **655** more pineapple tarts this week.

Solve the following word problems. Show your work in the space below.

1. Mia has 236 stickers. Abby has 127 fewer stickers than Mia.

    (a) How many stickers does Abby have?

    (b) How many stickers do they have altogether?

2. Roberto travels 3,280 mi. on his motorcycle. Steve travels 568 mi. farther than Roberto. How far do they travel altogether?

Singapore Math Level 3A & 3B

3. Hailey has 2,345 stamps in her collection. Asia has 3,542 stamps in her collection.

    (a) How many more stamps does Asia have than Hailey?

    (b) How many stamps do they have altogether?

4. Sarah earns $2,140 a month. Carmen earns $150 more than Sarah. Sonya earns $270 less than Carmen. How much does Sonya earn?

Singapore Math Level 3A & 3B

5. Rebecca pays $2,080 for her television set. Kimiko pays $275 less for her television set.

    (a) How much does Kimiko pay for her television set?

    (b) How much do both television sets cost?

6. 3,865 girls went to a concert. 1,459 more boys went to the same concert. How many children went to the concert altogether?

7. 2,015 people attended a carnival on Saturday. 3,585 more people attended the carnival on Sunday. How many people attended the carnival on both days?

8. Jason used 1,075 kg of cement to build a house on Monday. He used 360 kg less cement on Tuesday. How much cement did he use on both days?

9. A used van costs $5,180. It costs $3,960 to buy a used motorcycle.

(a) How much less is the used motorcycle than the used van?

(b) How much will it cost to buy the used van and the used motorcycle?

10. Alexandra spent $2,387 on books and school supplies last year. Her parents asked her to spend $500 less this year.

(a) How much could Alexandra spend on books and school supplies this year?

(b) If Alexandra were to spend $4,000 on books and school supplies this year, how much would she have overspent?

51

REVIEW 2

Solve the following subtraction problems. Show your work.

1.
```
  9,3 6 8
- 1,4 0 9
─────────
```

3.
```
  8,1 1 1
- 2,4 0 1
─────────
```

2.
```
  4,7 5 5
- 1,8 9 0
─────────
```

4.
```
  6,0 0 0
- 2,8 1 9
─────────
```

Write the missing number in each box.

5.
```
  9,5 □ 6
- 3,7 8 9
─────────
  5,7 4 7
```

6.
```
  □,5 4 4
- 1,1 7 3
─────────
  4,3 7 1
```

Fill in each blank with the correct answer.

7. Find the difference between 6,865 and 2,648.   _____

8. 2,865 − 1,750 = [   ]   _____

9. Subtract 1,011 from 5,900.   _____

10. 4,000 − 100 = [   ]   _____

Singapore Math Level 3A & 3B

11. Subtract 10 from 6,940.   _____

12. Find the difference between 8,000 and 450.   _____

13. 5,050 is 500 less than [   ].   _____

14. Solve the following problems to find Timothy's favorite sandwich.

R	6,3 8 9		T	2,4 1 5
	− 4,6 9 3			+ 1,5 9 6

E	8,2 0 0		A	5,1 8 9
	− 3,8 6 5			+ 2,6 9 0

U	3,4 8 7		B	4,4 4 4
	− 1,5 0 9			+ 2,0 5 5

N	7,7 7 7		P	1,0 9 0
	− 5,9 9 8			+ 2,8 9 5

[ ]	[ ]	[ ]	[ ]	[ ]	[ ]
3,985	4,335	7,879	1,779	1,978	4,011

[ ]	[ ]	[ ]	[ ]	[ ]	[ ]
6,499	1,978	4,011	4,011	4,335	1,696

Singapore Math Level 3A & 3B

Solve the following word problems. Show your work in the space below.

15. Sophia earns $2,470 a month. June earns $2,745 a month.

   (a) How much more money does June earn than Sophia?

   (b) How much do they earn altogether?

16. Yoko has 2,100 stamps in her collection. Andrew has 1,900 more stamps than Yoko. How many stamps do they have altogether?

Singapore Math Level 3A & 3B

17. Shop A sells 4,985 T-shirts in a month. Shop B sells 1,200 T-shirts more than Shop A. Shop C sells 2,350 fewer T-shirts than Shop B. How many T-shirts does Shop C sell?

18. Jake has 3,967 stickers. His brother gives him another 450 stickers. Jake then gives 1,050 stickers to his friends. How many stickers does Jake have left?

19. Raj drove 4,745 mi. in August. He drove 2,080 mi. less in September than in August. Find Raj's total driving distance in these 2 months.

Singapore Math Level 3A & 3B

20. Isaiah used 5,000 wooden blocks to build a castle. He used 4,360 fewer wooden blocks to build a house.

(a) How many wooden blocks did he use to build the house?

(b) How many wooden blocks did he use altogether?

Singapore Math Level 3A & 3B

Unit 5: MULTIPLYING NUMBERS BY 6, 7, 8, AND 9

Examples:

1. $8 \times 6 = \underline{\textbf{48}}$

2. $5 \times 7 = \underline{\textbf{35}}$

3. $8 \times 8 = \underline{\textbf{64}}$

4. $9 \times 3 = \underline{\textbf{27}}$

Fill in each blank with the correct answer.

1. $2 \times 6 = $ _____

2. $5 \text{ sixes} = $ _____

3. _____ $\times 8 = 80$

4. _____ $\times 7 = 56$

5. $9 \times 9 = $ _____

6. _____ $\times 8 = 40$

7. $4 \text{ eights} = $ _____

8. _____ $\times 6 = 24$

9. $3 \text{ sevens} = $ _____

10. $7 \times 7 = $ _____

11. $5 \times 9 = $ _____

12. _____ $\times 9 = 72$

13. _____ × 8 = 64

14. _____ × 8 = 48

15. 9 × 0 = _____

Match each steering wheel to the correct car.

16.  •

  •

17. •

  •

18. •

  •

19. •

  •

20. •

  •

Singapore Math Level 3A & 3B

Solve the following multiplication problems using the short-cut method.

21. (a) $7 \times 7 = 35 + \underline{\quad} + \underline{\quad}$

$ = 35 + \underline{\quad}$

$ = \underline{\quad}$

(b) $8 \times 6 = 30 + \underline{\quad} + \underline{\quad} + \underline{\quad}$

$ = 30 + \underline{\quad}$

$ = \underline{\quad}$

(c) $8 \times 8 = 40 + \underline{\quad} + \underline{\quad} + \underline{\quad}$

$ = 40 + \underline{\quad}$

$ = \underline{\quad}$

22. (a) $9 \times 8 = \underline{\quad} - \underline{\quad}$

$ = \underline{\quad}$

(b) $9 \times 6 = \underline{\quad} - \underline{\quad}$

$ = \underline{\quad}$

Study the pictures carefully. Fill in each blank with the correct answer.

23.

There are _____ groups of helmets.

There are _____ helmets in each group.

There are _____ helmets altogether.

24.

There are _____ groups of T-shirts.

There are _____ T-shirts in each group.

There are _____ T-shirts altogether.

Singapore Math Level 3A & 3B

25.

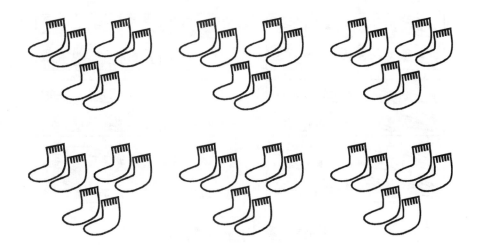

There are _____ groups of socks.

There are _____ socks in each group.

There are _____ socks altogether.

26.

There are _____ groups of spoons.

There are _____ spoons in each group.

There are _____ spoons altogether.

Singapore Math Level 3A & 3B

27.

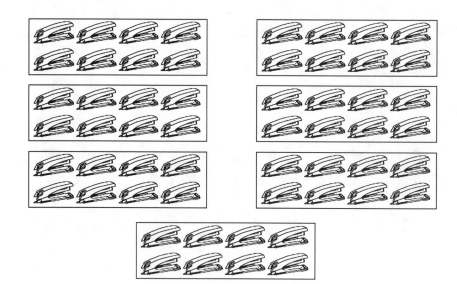

There are _____ groups of staplers.

There are _____ staplers in each group.

There are _____ staplers altogether.

Look at the pictures carefully. Write 2 multiplication and division sentences for each set of pictures.

28.

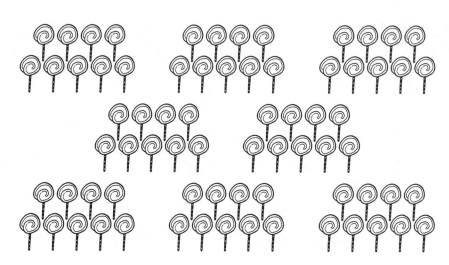

_____ × _____ = _____   _____ ÷ _____ = _____

_____ × _____ = _____   _____ ÷ _____ = _____

Singapore Math Level 3A & 3B

29.

_____ × _____ = _____   _____ ÷ _____ = _____

_____ × _____ = _____   _____ ÷ _____ = _____

30.

_____ × _____ = _____   _____ ÷ _____ = _____

_____ × _____ = _____   _____ ÷ _____ = _____

Singapore Math Level 3A & 3B

31.

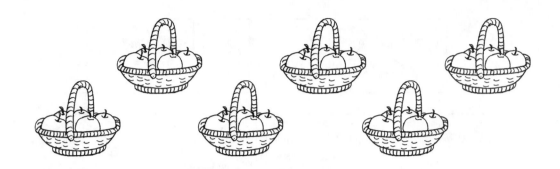

_____ × _____ = _____   _____ ÷ _____ = _____

_____ × _____ = _____   _____ ÷ _____ = _____

32.

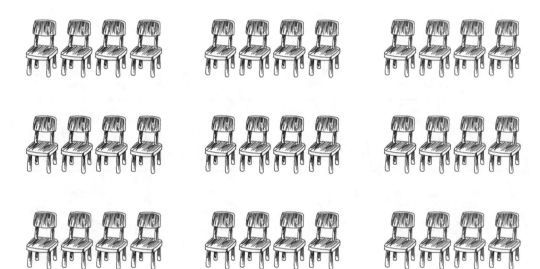

_____ × _____ = _____   _____ ÷ _____ = _____

_____ × _____ = _____   _____ ÷ _____ = _____

Singapore Math Level 3A & 3B

Solve the following word problems. Show your work in the space below.

33. Samantha bought 6 bags of oranges. There were 8 oranges in each bag. How many oranges did she buy altogether?

34. Andy buys 5 books at a bookshop. If each book costs $6, how much does Andy pay for all the books?

Singapore Math Level 3A & 3B

35. A group of people are going to the zoo by car. They need 7 cars altogether. If 5 people sit in each car, how many people are there in the group?

36. Elizabeth bakes 9 trays of muffins. There are 8 muffins on each tray. How many muffins does Elizabeth bake altogether?

37. Enzo has 42 stickers. He shares these stickers with 6 friends. How many stickers does each of them have?

38. Mrs. Arnold bought 64 apples. She put them equally into 8 bags. How many apples were there in each bag?

Singapore Math Level 3A & 3B

Unit 6: MULTIPLYING NUMBERS

Examples:

1.
```
    1 1
  ×   7
  ─────
    7 7
```

2.
```
      4
    3 5
  ×   8
  ─────
  2 8 0
```

3.
```
    2 1 0
  ×     3
  ───────
    6 3 0
```

4.
```
    1 3
    4 2 5
  ×     6
  ───────
  2,5 5 0
```

Solve the following multiplication problems. Show your work.

1.
```
    1 2
  ×   3
  ─────
```

2.
```
    1 1 2
  ×     4
  ───────
```

3.
```
    3 3
  ×   2
  ─────
```

4.
```
    2 1 0
  ×     2
  ───────
```

5.
```
    3 0 2
  ×     3
  ───────
```

6.
```
    4 4 2
  ×     2
  ───────
```

7.
```
    2 1 2
  ×     4
  ───────
```

8.
```
    3 1
  ×   3
  ─────
```

9.
```
    1 0 0
  ×     3
  ───────
```

10.
```
    1 2 1
  ×     4
  ───────
```

Singapore Math Level 3A & 3B

Match each door to the correct house.

11.
    49 × 5

12.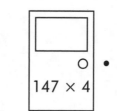
    147 × 4

13.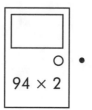
    94 × 2

14.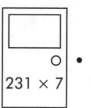
    231 × 7

15.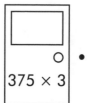
    375 × 3

16.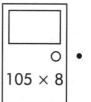
    105 × 8

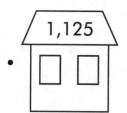
188

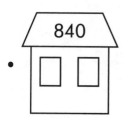
1,125

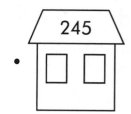
840

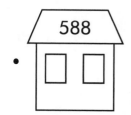
245

588

1,617

Singapore Math Level 3A & 3B

Fill in each box with the correct answer.

17.

	(a)		(f)			(b)		
(g)			(c)					
					(h)			
			(d)					
(i)		(j)			(e)			

Across	Down
(a) 112 × 8	(f) 91 × 7
(b) 79 × 9	(g) 102 × 6
(c) 62 × 5	(h) 46 × 8
(d) 214 × 4	(i) 98 × 9
(e) 118 × 7	(j) 80 × 8

73

Sandra is at the circus with her family. Find out who her favorite performer is.

18.

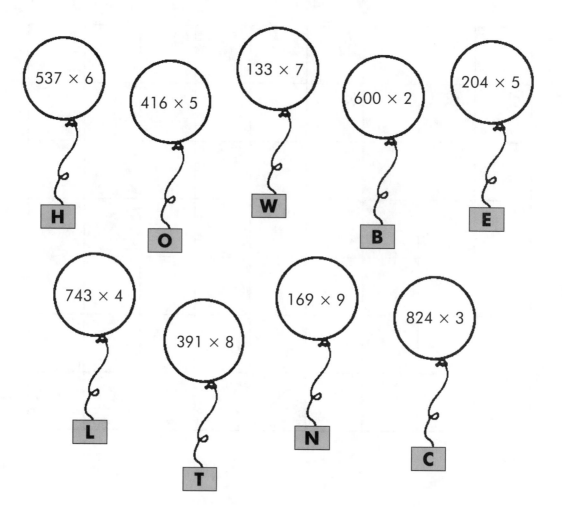

537×6
H

416×5
O

133×7
W

600×2
B

204×5
E

743×4
L

391×8
T

169×9
N

824×3
C

1,200	2,080	1,200	2,080		3,128	3,222	1,020

2,472	2,972	2,080	931	1,521

Singapore Math Level 3A & 3B

Solve the following word problems. Show your work in the space below.

19. Demetrius bought 6 boxes of colored pencils. There were 15 pencils in each box. How many colored pencils were there altogether?

20. 230 people went to a concert on Friday. If the daily number of people who went to the concert over the next 2 days was the same, what was the total number of people who went to the concert?

Singapore Math Level 3A & 3B

21. Sam bought 3 television sets at an electronics store. Each television set cost $637. How much did he spend at the electronics store?

22. Brittany bought 5 bottles of syrup at a supermarket. Each bottle contained 750 mL of syrup. Find the total volume of syrup that Brittany bought.

23. There were 153 cars in a parking lot. Each car had 4 wheels. How many wheels were there altogether?

REVIEW 3

Look at the pictures carefully. Fill in each blank with the correct answer.

1.

_____ × _____ = _____   _____ ÷ _____ = _____

_____ × _____ = _____   _____ ÷ _____ = _____

2.

_____ × _____ = _____   _____ ÷ _____ = _____

_____ × _____ = _____   _____ ÷ _____ = _____

77

Singapore Math Level 3A & 3B

Solve the following multiplication problems. Show your work.

3.
```
    1 4 7
  ×     8
  _____
```

5.
```
    6 3 2
  ×     4
  _____
```

4.
```
    3 1 2
  ×     3
  _____
```

6.
```
    5 0 0
  ×     3
  _____
```

Study the pictures carefully. Fill in each blank with the correct answer.

7.

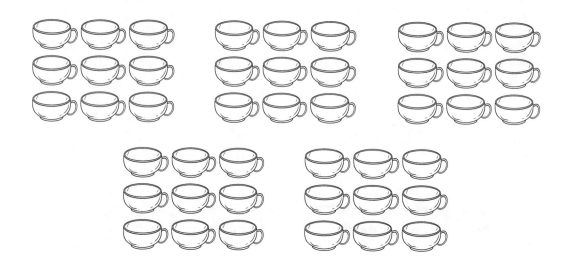

There are _____ groups of mugs.

There are _____ mugs in each group.

There are _____ mugs altogether.

Singapore Math Level 3A & 3B

Match each balloon to the correct girl.

8.

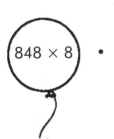
848 × 8 •

2,530

9.

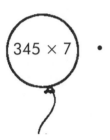
345 × 7 •

3,822

10.

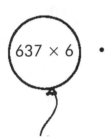
637 × 6 •

1,890

11.

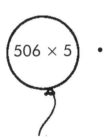
506 × 5 •

2,415

12.

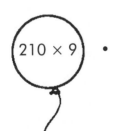
210 × 9 •

6,784

Singapore Math Level 3A & 3B

Fill in each blank with the correct answer.

13. 9 sixes = _____

14. _____ × 8 = 56

15. 4 × _____ = 28

16. _____ × 9 = 63

Solve the following word problems. Show your work in the space below.

17. Maddy uses 139 beads to make a bag. How many beads does she need to make 8 bags?

18. Vijay has 235 stamps in an album. He has 7 albums in his collection. How many stamps does he have altogether?

19. Ava bought 9 packets of ribbons. If there were 54 ribbons in all, how many ribbons were there in each packet?

20. If a car can transport 5 people, how many people can 45 cars transport?

Unit 7: DIVIDING NUMBERS

Examples:

1.
```
      2 1 2
  4 ) 8 4 8
      8
      ‾‾‾
        4
        4
        ‾‾‾
          8
          8
          ‾‾‾
          0
```

Quotient: **212**

Remainder: **0**

2.
```
      1 3 1
  7 ) 9 1 8
      7
      ‾‾‾
      2 1
      2 1
      ‾‾‾
          8
          7
          ‾‾‾
          1
```

Quotient: **131**

Remainder: **1**

Solve the following division problems. Show your work.

1. 7) 6 7

2. 5) 1 7

Quotient: _____

Remainder: _____

Quotient: _____

Remainder: _____

Singapore Math Level 3A & 3B

3. $3\overline{)25}$

6. $6\overline{)52}$

Quotient: _____

Remainder: _____

Quotient: _____

Remainder: _____

4. $9\overline{)88}$

7. $2\overline{)469}$

Quotient: _____

Remainder: _____

Quotient: _____

Remainder: _____

5. $4\overline{)29}$

8. $5\overline{)90}$

Quotient: _____

Remainder: _____

Quotient: _____

Singapore Math Level 3A & 3B

9. $3 \overline{)84}$

12. $6 \overline{)138}$

Quotient: _____

Quotient: _____

10. $8 \overline{)792}$

13. $3 \overline{)702}$

Quotient: _____

Quotient: _____

11. $7 \overline{)637}$

14. $9 \overline{)972}$

Quotient: _____

Quotient: _____

Singapore Math Level 3A & 3B

15. 4)812

Quotient: _____

16. Bryan is buying a birthday present for his brother. Solve the division problems to find out what the present is.

  2)17

  6)43

  8)55

  4)38

  7)60

Bryan's birthday present for his brother is a:

8 R 4	9 R 2	8 R 1	6 R 7	7 R 1	9 R 2

Singapore Math Level 3A & 3B

17. Solve the following division problems. Answer the question that follows.

R
22 ÷ 2 = ○
_____

S
48 ÷ 2 = ○
_____

M
39 ÷ 3 = ○
_____

H
48 ÷ 4 = ○
_____

O
20 ÷ 2 = ○
_____

U
64 ÷ 2 = ○
_____

What kind of room has no door?

___ ___ ___ ___ ___ ___ ___ ___
13   32   24   12   11   10   10   13

18. (a) List all the odd numbers from 1 to 9.

    _____

    (b) List all the even numbers from 1 to 9.

    _____

Singapore Math Level 3A & 3B

19. Circle all the even numbers in the box below.

33	48	56	97	45
16	74	82	20	

20. Cross out all the odd numbers in the box below.

11	8	65	83	37
20	49	7	91	52

21. What is the largest even number you can make using the digits 3, 0, 9, and 7?

_____

22. What is the smallest odd number you can make using the digits 4, 1, 5, and 2?

_____

Solve the following word problems. Show your work in the space below.

23. John bought 6 boxes of paperclips. He had 426 paperclips altogether. How many paperclips were there in each box?

Singapore Math Level 3A & 3B

24. A car manufacturer used 958 tires in June. If each car used 4 tires, how many cars did he manufacture in June?

25. Beatriz bakes 167 mini muffins. She gives all the muffins to her students. Each student gets 5 mini muffins.

    (a) How many students does she have in her class?

    (b) How many muffins does she have left?

Singapore Math Level 3A & 3B

Unit 8: PROBLEM SOLVING (MULTIPLYING AND DIVIDING)

Examples:

1. Mike saves $650 every month.

   (a) How much will he save in 9 months?

   (b) If he uses $962 to purchase a computer after 9 months, how much will he have left?

   (a)

$650	$650	$650	$650	$650	$650	$650	$650	$650

   ?

   $650 × 9 = $5,850

   He will save **$5,850** in 9 months.

   $$\begin{array}{r} \overset{4}{6}50 \\ \times\ \ \ 9 \\ \hline 5,850 \end{array}$$

   (b)

$962	?

   $5,850

   $5,850 − $962 = $4,888

   He will have **$4,888** left.

   $$\begin{array}{r} \overset{4}{\cancel{5}}\,\overset{17}{\cancel{8}}\,\overset{14}{\cancel{5}}\,\overset{10}{\cancel{0}} \\ -\ \ 962 \\ \hline 4,888 \end{array}$$

2. This year, Sierra and her aunt have a total age of 80. Her aunt is 4 times as old as Sierra.

   (a) How old is Sierra now?

   (b) How old is her aunt now?

   (a) Sierra [?]   } 80

   Her aunt [| | |]

   ?

   80 ÷ 5 = 16

   Sierra is **16** years old now.

   $$\begin{array}{r} 16 \\ 5\overline{)80} \\ \underline{5}\ \ \ \\ 30 \\ \underline{30} \\ 0 \end{array}$$

   (b) 16 × 4 = 64

   Her aunt is **64** years old now.

   $$\begin{array}{r} \overset{2}{1}6 \\ \times\ \ \ 4 \\ \hline 64 \end{array}$$

91

Singapore Math Level 3A & 3B

Solve the following word problems. Show your work in the space below.

1. Linh saved $135 in January. She saved twice as much in March. How much did Linh save in March?

2. Brooke bakes 484 dog biscuits. Annie bakes 4 times as many dog biscuits as Brooke. How many dog biscuits does Annie bake?

3. 187 people watched a movie on Wednesday. 3 times as many people watched the same movie over the weekend. How many people watched the movie that weekend?

Singapore Math Level 3A & 3B

4. Bakery A sold 565 loaves of bread. Bakery B sold twice as many loaves of bread as Bakery A. How many loaves of bread did Bakery B sell?

5. Cooper bought 8 packages of baseball cards. There were 25 cards in each package. How many baseball cards did he buy altogether?

6. Larry owns a fish farm. He bought 1,506 fish to be divided equally among his 3 ponds. How many fish could he put into each pond?

7. Alex spent $516 on transportation over 6 months. He spent an equal amount of money on transportation every month. How much did Alex spend on transportation each month?

8. Keiko has 679 beads. She uses 8 beads to make a ring.

   (a) How many rings can Keiko make?

   (b) How many beads are left?

9. Hasaan earns $1,375 a month. John earns $70 less than Hasaan. Luis earns twice as much as John.

    (a) How much does John earn?

    (b) How much does Luis earn?

10. There are 425 girls in a school. There are twice as many boys as girls.

    (a) How many boys are there?

95

(b)   How many students are there altogether?

11.   Sean collected 312 stamps last month. He collected 68 more stamps this month.

(a)   How many stamps did Sean collect this month?

(b)   How many stamps would each friend get if Sean's collection for this month was shared equally between his 2 friends?

12. Lauren spends $175 on food every month. Jade spends $159 on food every month.

   (a)   How much more money does Lauren spend on food than Jade?

   (b)   How much more money does Lauren spend on food than Jade in 6 months?

13. Mr. McKay travels 98 km from his home to the city. He travels the same distance back home.

   (a)   How far does Mr. McKay travel to and from the city?

(b) Mr. McKay has to travel to and from the city every day in a week. How far will he travel in all?

14. Emelda saved $160 every month for half a year. She then bought 8 presents with the money she saved.

(a) How much did Emelda save in half a year?

(b) What was the cost of each present if Emelda paid the same amount of money for all the presents?

Singapore Math Level 3A & 3B

15. Audrey sews 8 dresses in a week. Each dress uses 6 yd. of fabric.

    (a) How much fabric does she use in a week?

    (b) If she buys 100 yd. of fabric, how much fabric does she have left?

16. Kelly bought 9 packages of crayons. There were 25 crayons in each package. If Kelly were to give 5 crayons to each student, how many students did she have?

17. Kyra bought 3 crates of apples. There were 24 apples in each crate. She then bought 245 oranges. How many pieces of fruit did she buy altogether?

18. A radio costs $95. A television set costs $190. If Ken buys 2 radios and a television set, how much money does he need?

19. Charley bought a chair for $75. He then bought a table that cost 3 times as much as the chair. How much did Charley pay for the furniture?

20. Maria scored a total of 171 points in English and math. She scored twice as many points in English as she did in math. How many points did she score in English?

Unit 9: MENTAL CALCULATIONS

Examples:

1. Add 75 and 21 mentally.

   Step 1: 21 = 2 tens 1 one

   Step 2: 75 + 20 = 95

   Step 3: 95 + 1 = 96

   75 + 21 = **96**

2. Add 59 and 38 mentally.

   Step 1: 60 = 59 + 1

   Step 2: 60 + 38 = 98

   Step 3: 98 − 1 = 97

   59 + 38 = **97**

3. Subtract 26 from 67 mentally.

   Step 1: 26 = 2 tens 6 ones

   Step 2: 67 − 20 = 47

   Step 3: 47 − 6 = 41

   67 − 26 = **41**

4. Subtract 48 from 81 mentally.

   Step 1: 50 = 48 + 2

   Step 2: 81 − 50 = 31

   Step 3: 31 + 2 = 33

   81 − 48 = **33**

5. Find 6 × 90.

   6 × 90 = 6 × 9 tens = 54 tens = **540**

6. Find 4,900 ÷ 7.

   4,900 ÷ 7 = 49 hundreds ÷ 7 = 7 hundreds = **700**

Solve the following problems.

1. $65 + 24 = $ _____

2. $39 + 13 = $ _____

3. $56 + 78 = $ _____

4. $84 + 44 = $ _____

5. $74 + 25 = $ _____

6. $31 + 87 = $ _____

7. $42 + 48 = $ _____

8. $61 + 97 = $ _____

9. $57 + 29 = $ _____

10. $19 + 58 = $ _____

11. $49 - 18 = $ _____

12. $74 - 53 = $ _____

13. $64 - 19 = $ _____

14. $83 - 28 = $ _____

15. $37 - 9 = $ _____

16. $86 - 47 = $ _____

17. $62 - 35 = $ _____

18. $77 - 46 = $ _____

19. $96 - 47 = $ _____

20. $55 - 27 = $ _____

Singapore Math Level 3A & 3B

21. $5 \times 8 =$ _____

22. $9 \times 9 =$ _____

23. $7 \times 3 =$ _____

24. $3 \times 6 =$ _____

25. $4 \times 7 =$ _____

26. $2 \times 9 =$ _____

27. $8 \times 60 =$ _____

28. $6 \times 70 =$ _____

29. $3 \times 400 =$ _____

30. $5 \times 500 =$ _____

31. $24 \div 3 =$ _____

32. $54 \div 6 =$ _____

33. $50 \div 5 =$ _____

34. $72 \div 8 =$ _____

35. $90 \div 9 =$ _____

36. $80 \div 4 =$ _____

37. $350 \div 7 =$ _____

38. $210 \div 3 =$ _____

39. $360 \div 6 =$ _____

40. $160 \div 4 =$ _____

Singapore Math Level 3A & 3B

REVIEW 4

Solve the following division problems. Show your work.

1. $7\overline{)537}$

    Quotient: _____

    Remainder: _____

3. $9\overline{)908}$

    Quotient: _____

    Remainder: _____

2. $6\overline{)612}$

    Quotient: _____

4. $4\overline{)504}$

    Quotient: _____

5. What is the smallest 4-digit even number you can make using the digits 3, 5, 2, and 8?

    _____

6. What is the largest 4-digit odd number you can make using the digits 4, 8, 9, and 3?

    _____

7. Solve the following problems to find out where Joseph is going.

(I) 7)357   (R) 4)824

(B) 3)954   (A) 5)675

(Y) 6)714   (L) 9)711

___ ___ ___ ___ ___ ___ ___
79   51   318   206   135   206   119

8. Find the quotient when 278 is divided by 2.   _____

9. Add 37 and 69 mentally.   _____

10. List all the odd numbers from 50 to 60.

_____

11. Subtract 19 from 34 mentally.   _____

12. Find the quotient when 400 is divided by 8.   _____

Singapore Math Level 3A & 3B

13. List all the even numbers from 30 to 40.

_____

14. Find the product of 8 and 5 mentally. _____

15. Find the quotient when 24 is divided by 6. _____

Solve the following word problems. Show your work in the space below.

16. Serena buys 4 bags of noodles. There are 5 packets of noodles in each bag.

   (a) How many packets of noodles are there altogether?

   (b) Serena gives all the packets of noodles to her friends. If each of her friends receives 2 packets of noodles, how many friends does she give the noodles to?

Singapore Math Level 3A & 3B

17. Rashid has 6 albums of stamps. There are 230 stamps in each album. He gives the stamps to his 3 nephews. How many stamps does each nephew receive?

18. Anya uses 8 packets of sugar to bake 2 loaves of banana bread. Each packet of sugar has a mass of 50 g. How much sugar does she need for each loaf of banana bread?

19. Shop A sells 3 toys for $27. Shop B sells the same toys at 5 for $40. If Sadie wants to buy only 1 toy, which shop sells the toy at a cheaper price?

20. Nick travels a total of 464 yd. from his house to the city and back to his house.

    (a)   How far is Nick's house from the city?

    (b)   How far would Nick travel in 5 days if he were to travel from his house to the city and back to his house?

Singapore Math Level 3A & 3B

MID-REVIEW

Write the numbers on the lines.

1. seven thousand, three hundred   _____

2. four thousand, forty   _____

Write the following numbers as words on the lines.

3. 5,015   _____

4. 6,411   _____

Write the correct answers on the lines.

5. Find the sum of 3,618 and 2,934.   _____

6. Find the difference between 4,372 and 2,465.   _____

7. Multiply 149 by 7.   _____

8. Find the remainder when 863 is divided by 8.   _____

9. Add 16 and 25 mentally.   _____

Solve the following problems. Show your work.

10. $\begin{array}{r} 3{,}8\,9\,1 \\ +\ 4{,}6\,2\,3 \\ \hline \end{array}$

13. $\begin{array}{r} 8{,}2\,3\,0 \\ -\ 1{,}9\,6\,5 \\ \hline \end{array}$

11. $\begin{array}{r} 9{,}0\,0\,0 \\ -\ 4{,}5\,1\,5 \\ \hline \end{array}$

14. $\begin{array}{r} 4\,1\,4 \\ \times\quad 8 \\ \hline \end{array}$

12. $7\,\overline{)800}$

15. $4\,\overline{)312}$

16. Arrange these numbers in order. Begin with the smallest.

| 6,302, 4,263, 8,143, 2,436 |

———, ———, ———, ———

17. Fill in the blank with *greater* or *smaller*.

5,920 is _____ than 5,820.

Singapore Math Level 3A & 3B

18. Look at the picture carefully. Write 2 multiplication and division sentences.

_____ × _____ = _____   _____ ÷ _____ = _____

_____ × _____ = _____   _____ ÷ _____ = _____

19. Complete the number pattern.

2,017, _____, _____, 2,317, 2,417

20.

There are _____ groups of baskets.

There are _____ baskets in each group.

There are _____ baskets altogether.

Singapore Math Level 3A & 3B

Solve the following word problems. Show your work in the space below.

21. Rachel has 8 bags of seashells. There are 55 seashells in each bag. She then packs all the seashells into 2 bags equally. How many seashells are there in each bag?

22. Carson has 316 bottle caps. James has 3 times as many bottle caps as Carson. Dan has 400 fewer bottle caps than James. How many bottle caps does Dan have?

Singapore Math Level 3A & 3B

23. Amrita walks 1,416 yd. to the library from her house. She then goes to a shop which is 165 yd. from the library.

   (a) How far is the shop from her house?

   (b) Amrita walks to the library and to the shop from her house, using the same route home. How far does she walk?

Singapore Math Level 3A & 3B

24. The distance from Kovan City to Lakeview City is 138 km. There are 3 bus stops of equal distance between the 2 cities. If Olivia boards the bus at the first bus stop and gets off at the second bus stop, how far will she travel?

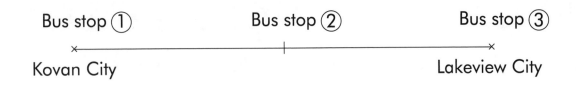

25. Monica paid $1,450 for a sofa. She paid twice as much for an entertainment center. If she gave the cashier $5,000, how much change would she receive?

CHALLENGE QUESTIONS

Solve the following problems on another sheet of paper.

1. The chart below shows the amount of money Simon saves from Monday to Wednesday.

Monday	Tuesday	Wednesday
$6	$12	$18

    If Simon continues to save in this pattern, how much money will he save by Sunday?

2. Complete the number pattern.

    3, 4, 7, 11, 18, 29, 47, _____, _____, _____

3. At a party, 6 handshakes were exchanged. Assuming that each person shook hands with another person once, how many people were at the party?

4. Form 2-digit numbers with the digits 1, 2, and 3. The digits in each number cannot be repeated. List all the 2-digit numbers that can be divided by 4.

5. Number X is a 4-digit even number. All its digits are different. The largest digit is in the tens place, and the smallest digit is in the hundreds place. The sum of the first 2 digits is 8 less than the sum of the last 2 digits. The sum of all its digits is 26. What is Number X if it is less than 6,000?

6. I am a number between 20 and 39. If I am divided by 5, there will be a remainder of 2. If I am divided by 6, there will be a remainder of 2. What number am I?

7. Complete the number pattern.

    2, 6, 10, 15, 20, 24, _____, _____, 38, 42, _____, _____

8. A group of 6 people shook hands with one another in a meeting. Each person shook hands with another person once. How many handshakes were exchanged?

9. When a bag of peaches is shared among 3 boys, there is 1 peach left. When the bag of peaches is shared among 4 boys, there is 1 peach left. How many peaches are there in the bag? (Assume that the number of peaches is not greater than 20.)

10. The first digit of a number is the same as the last digit. The second digit is 1 more than the first digit. The sum of all its digits is 4. Find the 3-digit odd number.

11. The chart below shows the number of workers and the number of days needed to build a 2-story building. Find the number of days needed for 10 workers to build the same building.

Number of workers	Number of days needed
50	32
40	44
30	56
20	68
10	?

12. When a book of 100 pages is opened, the sum of the facing page numbers can be divided by 5. The quotient is a product of 3 and 7. What are the facing page numbers?

3B LEARNING OUTCOMES

Unit 10 Money
Students should be able to
- add and subtract money in dollars and cents.
- solve story problems related to money.

Unit 11 Length, Mass, and Volume
Students should be able to
- state length in kilometers, meters, or centimeters.
- state mass in kilograms and grams.
- read the correct mass on scales.
- state volume in liters and milliliters.
- read the correct volume in measuring beakers.

Unit 12 Problem Solving (Length, Mass, and Volume)
Students should be able to
- solve story problems related to length, mass, and volume.

Review 5
This review tests students' understanding of Units 10, 11, & 12.

Unit 13 Bar Graphs
Students should be able to
- read and interpret data from bar graphs.
- draw bar graphs based on given data.

Unit 14 Fractions
Students should be able to
- recognize equivalent fractions.
- list up to the first eight equivalent fractions.
- complete equivalent fractions.
- state a fraction in its simplest form.
- compare and arrange fractions.
- add and subtract fractions.

Unit 15 Time
Students should be able to
- read and draw the correct time.
- state time in minutes or hours and minutes.
- find the length between two different times.
- find the starting time or ending time.
- add and subtract time in hours and minutes.
- solve story problems related to time.

Review 6
This review tests students' understanding of Units 13, 14, & 15.

Unit 16 Angles
Students should be able to
- identify angles and right angles.
- identify angles in 2-dimensional and 3-dimensional objects.
- identify the number of sides and angles in a figure.

Unit 17 Perpendicular and Parallel Lines
Students should be able to
- identify and draw perpendicular lines.
- identify and draw parallel lines.

Unit 18 Area and Perimeter
Students should be able to
- find the area of figures in cm^2, m^2, $in.^2$, or $ft.^2$.
- find the perimeter of figures.
- use the formula to find the area of figures.
- solve story problems related to area and perimeter.

Review 7
This review tests students' understanding of Units 16, 17, & 18.

Final Review
This review is an excellent assessment of students' understanding of all the topics in the second half of this book.

Singapore Math Level 3A & 3B

FORMULA SHEET

Unit 10 Money

Adding Money

There are three ways to add money.

❶ Add the dollars first.
Add the cents next.
Add the cents to the dollars.

Example: What is $10.20 + $28.35?

$$\$10 + \$28 = \$38$$
$$20¢ + 35¢ = 55¢$$
$$\$38 + 55¢ = \mathbf{\$38.55}$$

❷ Round up one of the addends (A) to the nearest dollar.
Add the other addend (B) and the round addend.
Subtract the difference between the round addend and addend (A) from the sum.

Example: What is $32.50 + $0.90?

$$\$32.50 + \$1 = \$33.50$$
$$\$33.50 - 10¢ = \mathbf{\$33.40}$$

❸ Add by formal algorithm.

Example: What is $61.80 + $12.70?

$$\begin{array}{r} \$6\overset{1}{1}.80 \\ +\ \$12.70 \\ \hline \mathbf{\$74.50} \end{array}$$

Make sure the dollar sign ($) and decimal point (.) align. If one of the addends does not have cents, add two zeros after the decimal point.

Subtracting Money

There are three ways to subtract money.

❶ Subtract the dollars first.
Subtract the cents next.
Add the cents to the dollars.

Example: What is $50.90 – $12.60?

$$\$50 - \$12 = \$38$$
$$90¢ - 60¢ = 30¢$$
$$\$38 + 30¢ = \mathbf{\$38.30}$$

❷ Round the second term (A) to the nearest dollar. Subtract the rounded term from the first term (B). Add the difference between the rounded amount and the original amount to the result.

Example: What is $49.60 – $8.70?

$$\begin{array}{cc} B & A \end{array}$$
$$\$49.60 - \$9 = \$40.60$$
$$\$40.60 + 30¢ = \mathbf{\$40.90}$$

❸ Add by formal algorithm.

Example: What is $88.00 – $54.60?

$$\begin{array}{r} \$8\overset{7}{8}.\overset{10}{0}0 \\ -\ \$54.60 \\ \hline \mathbf{\$33.40} \end{array}$$

Make sure the dollar sign ($) and decimal point (.) align. If one of the amounts does not have cents, add two zeros after the decimal point.

Unit 11 Length, Mass, and Volume

Length

Units of measurement: kilometers (km), meters (m), and centimeters (cm)

1 km = 1,000 m
1 m = 100 cm

Mass

Units of measurement: kilograms (kg) and grams (g)

1 kg = 1,000 g

When reading a scale,
• find how many grams or kilograms each small marking stands for,
• note the marking that the needle points to.

The marking pointed to by the needle shows the mass of an item.

Volume

Units of measurement: liters (L) and milliliters (mL)

1 L = 1,000 mL

Capacity is the total amount of liquid that a container can hold.
Volume is the amount of liquid in a container.

When reading the scale on a measuring container,
• find how many liters or milliliters each small marking stands for,
• note the liquid level that coincides with the marking on the measuring container.

The marking that coincides with the liquid level shows the capacity or volume of liquid in the measuring container.

Unit 12 Problem Solving (Length, Mass, and Volume)

Below is a suggested procedure when solving story problems.
1. Read the story problem carefully.
2. Find what you are supposed to solve in the story problem.
3. Draw model(s) for better understanding.
4. Write a number sentence. You have to write two number sentences when working on a two-step story problem.
5. Write the formal algorithm on the right side of the space.
6. Write a statement to answer the question in the story problem. You can underline the final answer in the statement.

Unit 13   Bar Graphs

A bar graph is a single chart that displays bars representing certain values along its axis.

Bar graphs organize data effectively. This helps in easy comparison and problem solving.

When interpreting data from bar graphs, note the scale of the axis.

Two types of bar graphs are introduced in this book. They are vertical and horizontal bar graphs.

An example of a vertical bar graph is shown below.

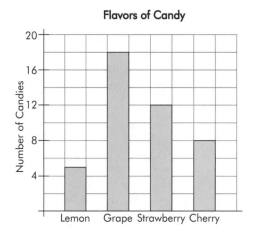

An example of a horizontal bar graph is shown below.

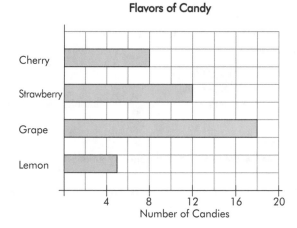

Unit 14   Fractions

Equivalent fractions are fractions that have the same value.

Examples: $\frac{1}{3}$, $\frac{2}{6}$, $\frac{3}{9}$, and $\frac{4}{12}$

In order to find an equivalent fraction, multiply both the numerator and denominator of a fraction by the same number.

Example: $\frac{3 \times 2}{5 \times 2} = \frac{6}{10}$

Comparing fractions

- When fractions have the same denominator, just compare their numerators.
  The greater the numerator, the greater the fraction.

- When fractions have the same numerator, just compare their denominators.
  The greater the denominator, the smaller the fraction.

- When fractions do not have the same denominator, make these fractions equivalent first.
  It is easier to compare when the fractions have the same denominator.

Adding fractions

1. Make sure all addends have the same denominator.
   If they do not, find the equivalent fractions.
2. Add all numerators of each fraction to get the result.
3. Write the final fraction in its simplest form if required.

Subtracting fractions

1. Make sure all terms have the same denominator.
   If they do not, find the equivalent fractions.

   A whole (1) can be expressed in equivalent fractions like $\frac{2}{2}$, $\frac{3}{3}$, $\frac{4}{4}$, $\frac{5}{5}$, $\frac{6}{6}$, $\frac{7}{7}$, $\frac{8}{8}$, $\frac{9}{9}$, $\frac{10}{10}$, $\frac{11}{11}$, and $\frac{12}{12}$.
2. Subtract all numerators of each fraction to get the result.
3. Write the final fraction in its simplest form if required.

Unit 15   Time

Telling time

When the minute hand points before/to 6 on the face of a clock, use the word *after*.

When using the word *after*, count the minutes that are past a certain hour.

Example:

10:20 is **20 minutes after 10**.

When the minute hand has moved past 6 on the face of a clock, use the word *to*.

When using the word *to*, count the minutes needed to move to the next hour.

Example:

12:45 is **15 minutes to 1**.

Converting hours and minutes

1 hour = 60 minutes

- When converting hours to minutes, multiply the number of hours by 60.
  Example: 7 hr. = 7 × 60 min. = 420 min.

- When converting minutes to hours, divide the number of hours by 60.
  Example: 540 min. = 540 min. ÷ 60 min. = 9 hr.

Adding time

1. Add the minutes. If the total is more than 60, regroup the hours and minutes.
2. Add the hours. Remember to add an hour from the regrouping if necessary.

Singapore Math Level 3A & 3B

Subtracting time
1. Subtract the minutes. If this is not possible, regroup the hours and minutes.
2. Subtract the hours.

Finding the length of time
A timeline is used to find the length of time in minutes and hours. It can also be used to find the time before/after a certain time.

Example:

There are **2 hr. 20 min.** from 4:30 P.M. to 6:50 P.M.
2 hr. 20 min. before 6:50 P.M. is **4:30 P.M.**
2 hr. 20 min. after 4:30 P.M. is **6:50 P.M.**

Unit 16   Angles
When two straight lines meet, an angle is formed.

Example:

A right angle is formed when a vertical line meets a horizontal line.

Symbol: ¬

Example:

The size of the angle is measured in degrees. A right angle measures 90 degrees.

Angles can be found in 2-dimensional shapes and 3-dimensional objects.
The number of sides of a 2-dimensional shape and the number of angles in that shape are usually the same.

Example:

This 2-dimensional shape has 4 sides and 4 angles.

Unit 17   Perpendicular and Parallel Lines
When two straight lines meet and form a right angle, these two lines are known as **perpendicular lines**.

Symbol: ⊥

Examples:

When drawing perpendicular lines,
1. draw two straight lines with a ruler,
2. make sure a right angle is formed when these two lines meet.

When two straight lines are equal distance away from each other and do not meet, they are known as **parallel lines**.

Symbol: //

Examples:

When drawing parallel lines,
1. draw two straight lines with a ruler,
2. make sure one line is equal distance away from the other line at all points.

Unit 18   Area and Perimeter
Area
Area is defined as the size of a surface.
Units of measurement: square centimeters (cm²), square meters (m²), square inches (in.²), and square feet (ft.²).

Finding area of a figure in a grid of 1-cm and 1-in. squares
Count the number of squares that make up the figure.

Finding area of a rectangle
Area = Length × Width
Make sure the units of measurement for both length and width are the same.

Finding area of a square
Area = Length × Length
Make sure the units of measurement for all four sides are the same.

Perimeter
Perimeter is defined as the distance around a figure or an object.
Units of measurement: centimeters (cm), meters (m), inches (in.), and feet (ft.)

Finding perimeter of a figure in a grid of 1-cm and 1-in. squares
Count the number of lines that make up the figure.

Finding perimeter of a rectangle
Add the length of its four sides.

Finding perimeter of a square
Add the length of its four sides.
Alternatively, multiply the length of one side by 4 as all sides of a square are equal.

Singapore Math Level 3A & 3B

Unit 10: MONEY

Examples:

1. What is $27.35 + $12.35?

   $27 + $12 = $39

   35¢ + 35¢ = 70¢

   $39 + 70¢ = **$39.70**

2. What is $98.50 − $14.90?

   $98.50 − $15.00 = $83.50

   $83.50 + 10¢ = **$83.60**

3. Jessie starts with $25. She spends $6.90 on a notebook and $2.80 on a pen. How much money does Jessie have left?

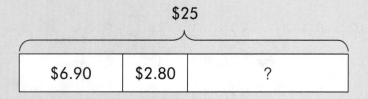

$25

| $6.90 | $2.80 | ? |

   $6.90 + $2.80 = $9.70

   $25.00 − $9.70 = $15.30

Jessie has **$15.30** left.

Write the correct answers on the lines.

1. $\$5.35 + \$3.00 = \$\underline{\hspace{2cm}}$

2. $\$43.20 + \$8.00 = \$\underline{\hspace{2cm}}$

3. $\$14.00 + \$90.75 = \$\underline{\hspace{2cm}}$

4. $\$30.00 + \$68.90 = \$\underline{\hspace{2cm}}$

5. $\$9.05 + \$0.55 = \$\underline{\hspace{2cm}}$

6. $\$24.00 + \$0.90 = \$\underline{\hspace{2cm}}$

7. $\$0.80 + \$70.00 = \$\underline{\hspace{2cm}}$

8. $\$82.40 + \$6.80 = \$\underline{\hspace{2cm}}$

9. $\$53.60 + \$2.25 = \$\underline{\hspace{2cm}}$

10. $\$43.50 + \$1.80 = \$\underline{\hspace{2cm}}$

Fill in each blank with the correct answer.

Example:
$$\$25.40 + \$0.90 = \$25.40 + \$1.00$$
$$= \$26.40 - 10¢$$
$$= \underline{\$26.30}$$

---

11. $\$18.20 + \$0.70 = \$\underline{\hspace{1.5cm}} + \$\underline{\hspace{1.5cm}}$

$= \$\underline{\hspace{1.5cm}} - \underline{\hspace{1.5cm}}¢$

$= \$\underline{\hspace{1.5cm}}$

126

Singapore Math Level 3A & 3B

12. $26.90 + $0.80 = $_____ + $_____

   = $_____ – _____¢

   = $_____

13. $72.50 + $0.90 = $_____ + $_____

   = $_____ – _____¢

   = $_____

14. $59.60 + $0.80 = $_____ + $_____

   = $_____ – _____¢

   = $_____

15. $76.40 + $0.70 = $_____ + $_____

   = $_____ – _____¢

   = $_____

Solve the addition problems below. Show your work.

16.　　$ 2 3 . 5 0
　　 + $ 1 3 . 2 0
　　 _____

18.　　$ 5 1 5 . 5 5
　　 + $　 7 9 . 2 5
　　 _____

17.　　$ 8 6 . 7 5
　　 + $ 3 7 . 4 5
　　 _____

19.　　　$ 4 . 3 5
　　 +　 $ 0 . 9 0
　　 _____

Singapore Math Level 3A & 3B

20.　　　$ 7 3 . 2 0
　　　+ $ 1 8 . 0 0
　　　_____

23.　　　$ 5 6 . 2 0
　　　+ $ 6 4 . 1 5
　　　_____

21.　　　$ 1 2 5 . 8 0
　　　+ $ 2 1 4 . 4 0
　　　_____

24.　　　$ 4 9 . 7 0
　　　+ $ 2 8 . 5 0
　　　_____

22.　　　$ 2 1 7 . 0 0
　　　+ $ 1 4 2 . 8 5
　　　_____

25.　　　$ 6 7 . 9 0
　　　+ $ 1 7 . 7 0
　　　_____

Write the correct answers on the lines.

26.　$39.40 – $5.00 = $_____

27.　$78.55 – $4.00 = $_____

28.　$36.70 – $0.60 = $_____

29.　$82.75 – $0.20 = $_____

30.　$48.60 – $0.45 = $_____

31.　$99.50 – $0.35 = $_____

32.　$87.30 – $4.10 = $_____

33.　$69.55 – $3.35 = $_____

34.　$92.60 – $1.30 = $_____

35.　$58.80 – $7.50 = $_____

Fill in each blank with the correct answer.

> *Example:*
> $$\$80.50 - \$0.90 = \$80.50 - \$1.00$$
> $$= \$79.50 + 10¢$$
> $$= \underline{\$79.60}$$

36. $67.40 − $0.80 = $_____ − $_____

                   = $_____ + _____¢

                   = $_____

37. $46.20 − $0.70 = $_____ − $_____

                   = $_____ + _____¢

                   = $_____

38. $28.30 − $0.90 = $_____ − $_____

                   = $_____ + _____¢

                   = $_____

39. $70.60 − $0.80 = $_____ − $_____

                   = $_____ + _____¢

                   = $_____

40. $45.20 − $0.90 = $_____ − $_____

                   = $_____ + _____¢

                   = $_____

Singapore Math Level 3A & 3B

Solve the subtraction problems below. Show your work.

41.
$$\begin{array}{r} \$\,7.80 \\ -\ \$\,3.50 \\ \hline \end{array}$$

46.
$$\begin{array}{r} \$\,143.05 \\ -\ \$\ \ 21.80 \\ \hline \end{array}$$

42.
$$\begin{array}{r} \$\,50.00 \\ -\ \$\ \ 5.60 \\ \hline \end{array}$$

47.
$$\begin{array}{r} \$\,955.60 \\ -\ \$\ \ 89.45 \\ \hline \end{array}$$

43.
$$\begin{array}{r} \$\,280.50 \\ -\ \$\ \ 66.60 \\ \hline \end{array}$$

48.
$$\begin{array}{r} \$\,49.25 \\ -\ \$\ \ 5.60 \\ \hline \end{array}$$

44.
$$\begin{array}{r} \$\,23.10 \\ -\ \$\ \ 2.30 \\ \hline \end{array}$$

49.
$$\begin{array}{r} \$\,10.00 \\ -\ \$\ \ 3.45 \\ \hline \end{array}$$

45.
$$\begin{array}{r} \$\,758.70 \\ -\ \$\,329.40 \\ \hline \end{array}$$

50.
$$\begin{array}{r} \$\,659.20 \\ -\ \$\ \ 92.25 \\ \hline \end{array}$$

Singapore Math Level 3A & 3B

51. Below are some items sold in a store.

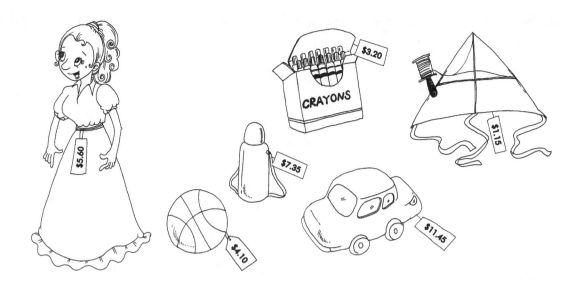

(a) Janice bought a box of crayons and a doll. How much did she pay altogether?

$ _____

(b) Maggie bought a doll and a water bottle. How much did she pay for the items?

$ _____

(c) Paul had only $5. List the two things that Paul could buy with that amount of money.

_____

(d) Mike bought a toy car and a kite. He gave the cashier $20. How much change would he receive?

$ _____

(e) How much more did the water bottle cost than the ball?

$ _____

Singapore Math Level 3A & 3B

Solve the following story problems. Show your work in the space below.

52. Ashley buys a can of orange juice for $1.10 and a box of cereal for $3.50. How much does Ashley pay altogether?

53. Karly bought a pair of shoes and two blouses for $75.35. If she gave the cashier $100, how much change would she receive?

54. Desmond gave $500 to his parents. His brother gave them $200 more than Desmond. How much did his parents receive altogether?

Singapore Math Level 3A & 3B

55. Carmen spends $75.70 on her phone bill, $125 on her car, and $360 on food each month. How much does she spend altogether each month?

56. Amanda pays $750 for a table and five matching chairs. If the table costs $200, how much do the chairs cost?

57. Beth saved $500 in January. She saved $350 in February. She needed to save $1,000 by March. How much did Beth have to save in March?

58. Josie bought an electronic toy for $34.90. She gave the cashier 4 10-dollar bills. How much change should she receive?

59. After Andy spent $80.35 and Aaron spent $43.60, both had the same amount of money left.

(a) If Andy had $19.65 left, how much money did Aaron have at first?

(b) How much more money did Andy have than Aaron?

Singapore Math Level 3A & 3B

Unit 11: LENGTH, MASS, AND VOLUME

Examples:

1. State the number of meters in 7 km 56 m.

   7 km 56 m = 7,000 m + 56 m

   $\qquad\quad$ = **7,056 m**

   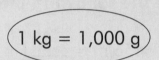

2. State the number of kilograms and grams in 6,004 g.

   6,004 g = 6,000 g + 4 g

   $\qquad\quad$ = **6 kg 4 g**

   1 kg = 1,000 g

3. The two measuring beakers show the capacity of Container A.

   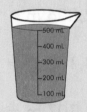 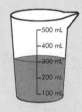

   $\qquad$ 500 mL + 300 mL = 800 mL

   The capacity of Container A is **800 mL**.

State the following measurements in meters and centimeters.

1. 323 cm = _____ m _____ cm

2. 710 cm = _____ m _____ cm

3. 805 cm = _____ m _____ cm

4. 1,000 cm = _____ m _____ cm

5. 1,525 cm = _____ m _____ cm

6. 521 cm = _____ m _____ cm

7. 606 cm = _____ m _____ cm

8. 2,156 cm = _____ m _____ cm

9. 43 cm = _____ m _____ cm

10. 2,336 cm = _____ m _____ cm

135

State the following measurements in centimeters.

11. 4 m 34 cm = _____ cm

12. 1 m 10 cm = _____ cm

13. 10 m 5 cm = _____ cm

14. 6 m 56 cm = _____ cm

15. 20 m = _____ cm

16. 8 m 8 cm = _____ cm

17. 15 m 30 cm = _____ cm

18. 7 m 89 cm = _____ cm

19. 31 m 40 cm = _____ cm

20. 9 m 45 cm = _____ cm

State the following measurements in kilometers and meters.

21. 1,456 m = ____ km ____ m

22. 6,830 m = ____ km ____ m

23. 1,000 m = ____ km ____ m

24. 6,592 m = ____ km ____ m

25. 9,225 m = ____ km ____ m

26. 4,050 m = ____ km ____ m

27. 8,003 m = ____ km ____ m

28. 2,006 m = ____ km ____ m

29. 3,100 m = ____ km ____ m

30. 7,707 m = ____ km ____ m

State the following measurements in meters.

31. 3 km 850 m = _____ m

32. 1 km 70 m = _____ m

33. 5 km = _____ m

34. 9 km 220 m = _____ m

35. 12 km 500 m = _____ m

36. 27 km 3 m = _____ m

37. 9 km 90 m = _____ m

38. 20 km 100 m = _____ m

39. 2 km 300 m = _____ m

40. 1 km 309 m = _____ m

Study the map below and answer the following questions.

41.

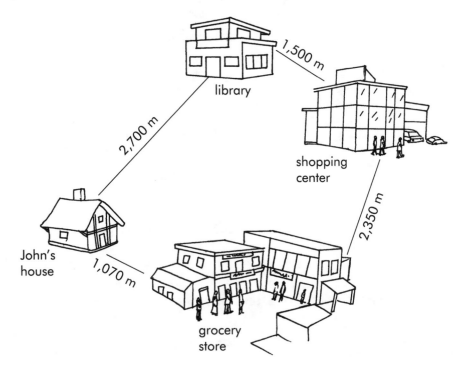

(a) The library is _____ m away from John's house.

It is _____ km _____ m away from John's house.

(b) The grocery store is _____ m away from the shopping center.

It is _____ km _____ m away from the shopping center.

(c) The shopping center is _____ m away from the library.

It is _____ km _____ m away from the library.

(d) The grocery store is _____ m away from John's house.

It is _____ km _____ m away from John's house.

Fill in each blank with cm, m, or km.

42. The marathon is 42 ____.

43. The pencil is 15 ____.

44. Bella is 142 ____ tall.

45. The tree is 1 ____ tall.

Singapore Math Level 3A & 3B

State the following measurements in grams.

46. 1 kg = _____ g

47. 1 kg 238 g = _____ g

48. 3 kg 300 g = _____ g

49. 9 kg 569 g = _____ g

50. 5 kg 955 g = _____ g

51. 7 kg 67 g = _____ g

52. 10 kg 760 g = _____ g

53. 4 kg 8 g = _____ g

54. 8 kg 642 g = _____ g

55. 2 kg 484 g = _____ g

State the following measurements in kilograms and grams.

56. 1,369 g = ____ kg ____ g

57. 4,820 g = ____ kg ____ g

58. 12,790 g = ____ kg ____ g

59. 6,606 g = ____ kg ____ g

60. 10,001 g = ____ kg ____ g

61. 3,033 g = ____ kg ____ g

62. 5,115 g = ____ kg ____ g

63. 8,780 g = ____ kg ____ g

64. 2,200 g = ____ kg ____ g

65. 9,090 g = ____ kg ____ g

Read the scales. Write the correct answers on the lines.

66.

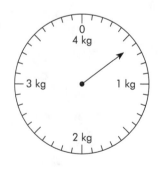

_____ g

67.

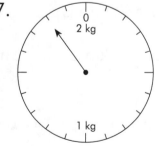

_____ g

Singapore Math Level 3A & 3B

68.

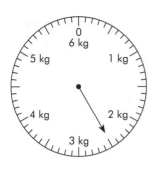

_____ g

70.

_____ g

69.

_____ g

71.

_____ g

Fill in each blank with _g_ or _kg_.

72. The mass of an apple is 180 _____.

73. The mass of David is 29 _____.

74. The mass of an elephant is 5,000 _____.

75. The mass of a book is 325 _____.

Singapore Math Level 3A & 3B

For each question, look at the measuring beaker(s) carefully. They are used to fill different containers. Write the correct capacity of the container in each blank.

76.

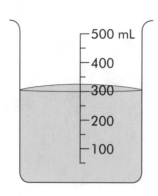

The capacity of the container is _____ mL.

77.

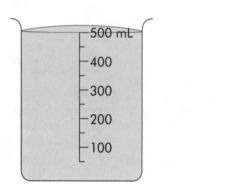 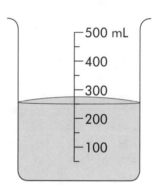

The capacity of the container is _____ mL.

78.

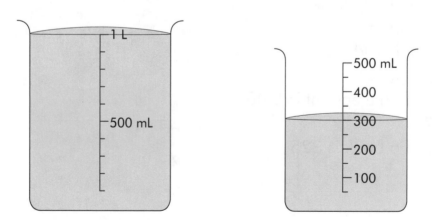

The capacity of the container is _____ L _____ mL.

Singapore Math Level 3A & 3B

79.

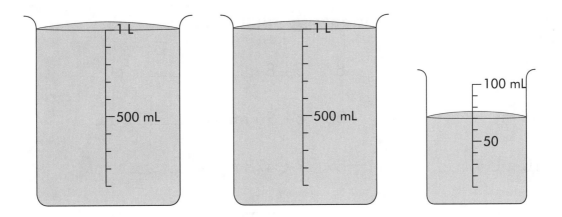

The capacity of the container is _____ L _____ mL.

80.

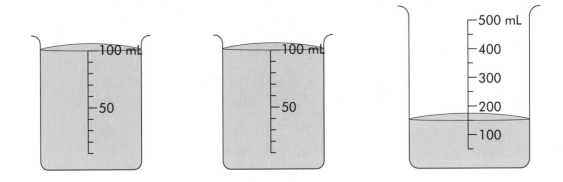

The capacity of the container is _____ mL.

81.

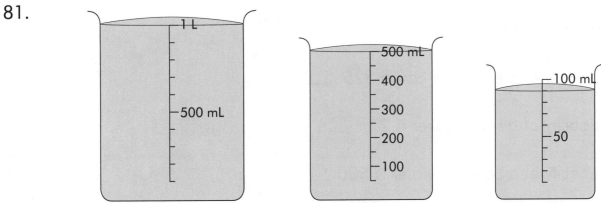

The capacity of the container is _____ L _____ mL.

Singapore Math Level 3A & 3B

State the following measurements in milliliters.

82. 1 L = _____ mL   87. 3 L 8 mL = _____ mL

83. 4 L 368 mL = _____ mL   88. 8 L 96 mL = _____ mL

84. 10 L 10 mL = _____ mL   89. 7 L 478 mL = _____ mL

85. 8 L 818 mL = _____ mL   90. 9 L 9 mL = _____ mL

86. 12 L 200 mL = _____ mL   91. 11 L 110 mL = _____ mL

State the following measurements in liters and milliliters.

92. 4,352 mL = ___ L ___ mL   97. 5,015 mL = ___ L ___ mL

93. 9,909 mL = ___ L ___ mL   98. 7,007 mL = ___ L ___ mL

94. 3,100 mL = ___ L ___ mL   99. 6,060 mL = ___ L ___ mL

95. 8,702 mL = ___ L ___ mL   100. 10,001 mL = ___ L ___ mL

96. 2,000 mL = ___ L ___ mL   101. 1,100 mL = ___ L ___ mL

Fill in each blank with *mL* or *L*.

102. The capacity of a soft drink can is 325 ___.

103. The capacity of a slow cooker is 2 ___.

104. The capacity of a bottle of water is 500 ___.

105. The capacity of a fish tank is 10 ___.

Unit 12: PROBLEM SOLVING (LENGTH, MASS, AND VOLUME)

Examples:

1. Jose draws 5 buckets of water from a well. He fills each bucket to the brim with water. The capacity of each bucket is 3 L. How many liters of water does Jose draw from the well?

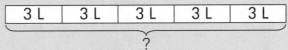

$$5 \times 3 = 15$$

Jose draws **15 L** of water from the well.

2. The distance between Greenland Mall and Sunshine Fitness Center is 1 km 250 m. The distance between the library and Sunshine Fitness Center is 1 km 50 m. Rafi walks from Greenland Mall, past the Sunshine Fitness Center, to the library. After borrowing books from the library, he walks back to Sunshine Fitness Center. What is the total distance Rafi has walked?

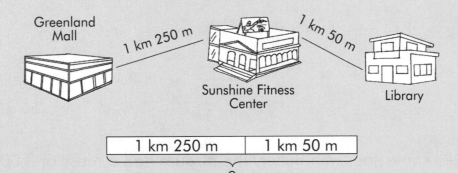

1 km 250 m + 1 km 50 m = 2 km 300 m

Rafi walks a distance of 2 km 300 m from Greenland Mall to the library.

$$\begin{array}{r} 1,\overset{1}{2}50 \\ +\ 1,050 \\ \hline 2,300 \end{array}$$

2 km 300 m + 1 km 50 m = 3 km 350 m

The total distance Rafi has walked is **3 km 350 m**.

$$\begin{array}{r} 2,300 \\ +\ 1,050 \\ \hline 3,350 \end{array}$$

Solve the following story problems. Show your work in the space below.

1. A pole is longer than a wooden plank by 88 cm. If the pole is 325 cm, what is the length of the wooden plank?

2. A ribbon 840 cm long is cut into 5 equal pieces. What is the length of each piece of ribbon?

3. Jonah's mass is 38 kg and Haruka's mass is 37 kg. What is their total mass?

4. Sarah mixed some flour with butter. The mixture had a mass of 3,000 g. If she used 900 g of butter, how much flour did she use? State your answer in kilograms and grams.

Singapore Math Level 3A & 3B

5. Mandy prepares 10,360 mL of latte. If she uses 7,900 mL of coffee, how much milk does she add?

6. Sharon's car has a tank capacity of 40 L. How much gasoline has she used up if there are 18 L of gasoline left in her tank? Assume that she fills her car up with gasoline every time.

7. Ms. Drew bought a box of crackers. The mass of the box of crackers was 1,800 g. She packed the crackers into 3 equal bags. What was the mass of each bag of crackers?

8. Grace bought a dozen similar cans of orange juice. If the capacity of each can of orange juice was 550 mL, how much orange juice did she buy? State your answer in liters and milliliters.

Singapore Math Level 3A & 3B

9. The total length of three sticks is 555 cm. If two of the sticks measure a total of 272 cm, what is the length of the third stick? State your answer in meters and centimeters.

10. A chair has a mass of 2,700 g. A table has a mass of 3,960 g. How much heavier is the table than the chair?

11. The length of a garden is 8 m and its width is 6 m. If John wants to put up a fence around the garden, how long will the fence be?

12. Basir's bag of groceries has a mass of 4,870 g. His bag of groceries is 3,560 g heavier than Andy's. What is the mass of Andy and Basir's bags of groceries? State your answer in kilograms and grams.

13. A fish market sold 30,960 g of fish on Saturday. It sold 10,040 g of fish on Sunday. How much fish did the market sell on both days? State your answer in kilograms and grams.

Singapore Math Level 3A & 3B

14. Sam bought 8,300 mL of paint. Evan bought 6,970 mL less of paint. How much paint did they buy altogether?

15. Kelly used 125 g of flour to make pastries. Her sister used 5 times as much flour to bake cakes. How much more flour did her sister use than Kelly? State your answer in grams.

16. Tree A is 135 cm. Tree B is 3 times taller than Tree A. What is the total height of both trees?

17. Andre has to paint a wall of 15 m by 3 m. Tim has to paint another wall of 12 m by 4 m.

    (a) Who has to paint more wall space?

    (b) How much more wall space does he have to paint?

Singapore Math Level 3A & 3B

18.

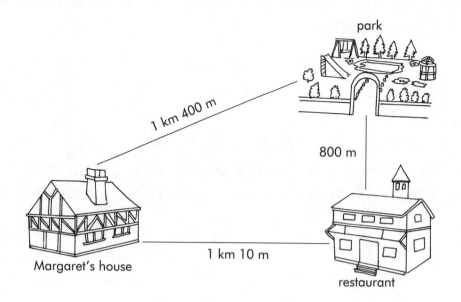

Margaret walked from her house to the park and then to the restaurant. She then walked home from the restaurant. What was the total distance walked by Margaret? State your answer in kilometers and meters.

19. Jake uses 6,500 mL of water on Monday. His brother uses 2,765 mL of water more than Jake. How much water do both of them use? State your answer in liters and milliliters.

20. Joshua poured a bottle of milk into 8 glasses and had a remaining 250 mL of milk.

   (a) If each glass of milk had a volume of 420 mL, find the total volume of the 8 glasses of milk.

   (b) How much milk was there in all? State your answer in liters and milliliters.

21. A waiter filled some pots of coffee to the brim. Each pot could hold 2 L of coffee.

   (a) If the waiter had 14 L of coffee, how many pots of coffee could he fill?

   (b) If the waiter had 2 pots of coffee left after breakfast, how many pots of coffee were used?

149

REVIEW 5

Fill in each blank with the correct answer.

1. (a) 415 cm = _____ m _____ cm   (b) 830 cm = _____ m _____ cm

2. (a) 6,269 m = _____ km _____ m   (b) 5,500 m = _____ km _____ m

3. (a) 7,670 g = _____ kg _____ g   (b) 4,008 g = _____ kg _____ g

4. (a) 4,835 mL = _____ L _____ mL   (b) 6,505 ml = _____ L _____ mL

5. (a) 6 km 975 m = _____ m   (b) 8 km 8 m = _____ m

6. (a) 9 m 5 cm = _____ cm   (b) 10 m = _____ cm

7. (a) 2 L 2 mL = _____ mL   (b) 5 L 275 mL = _____ mL

8. (a) 2 kg 636 g = _____ g   (b) 5 kg 30 g = _____ g

9.

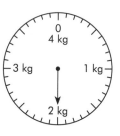

The mass of a watermelon is _____ g.

10.

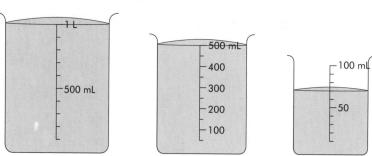

The capacity of a water bottle is _____ mL.

Singapore Math Level 3A & 3B

11. Below are some items sold at a bakery.

(a) Angie buys a loaf of bread and a piece of cake. How much does she pay altogether?

$_____

(b) Samantha buys 2 buns. She gives the cashier $5. How much change will she receive?

$_____

(c) Tony buys four 1-kg cakes and a doughnut. How much does he pay in all?

$_____

12. Study the map below carefully and answer the following questions.

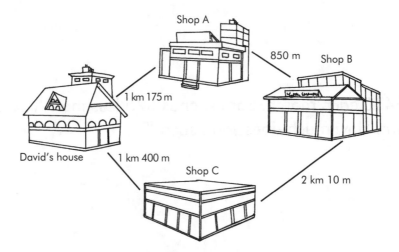

(a) Shop A is _____ m away from Shop B.

(b) Shop C is _____ m away from David's house.

(c) The distance between David's house and Shop A is _____ m.

Singapore Math Level 3A & 3B

Solve the following story problems. Show your work in the space below.

13. Ken gives $500 of his salary to his parents. He spends $375 and saves the rest. If he earns $1,200 every month, how much does Ken save?

14. Benjamin jogs twice daily. He jogs a distance of 8 km 120 m each time. How far does Benjamin jog daily? Write your answer in kilometers and meters.

15. Alex spends $410 each month. Sam spends $75 less than Alex. John spends $160 more than Sam. How much does John spend?

Singapore Math Level 3A & 3B

16. Greg mixes 4 kg 360 g of cement with 2 kg 500 g of sand.

    (a) How much more cement does he mix? Write your answer in kilograms and grams.

    (b) What is the total mass of the mixture? Write your answer in kilograms and grams.

17. The total length of two poles is 5 m 70 cm. Pole A is 2 m 25 cm long.

    (a) Which pole is longer, A or B?

    (b) How much longer? Write your answer in centimeters.

Singapore Math Level 3A & 3B

18. Zoe bought four cartons of milk. If each carton of milk was 250 mL, what was the total volume of the four cartons of milk? Write your answer in liters.

19. Sam pays $10.00 for some oranges, apples, and pears. If the apples cost $3.60 and the pears cost $3.55, how much do the oranges cost?

20. Mandy made 3 L 250 mL of orange juice on Monday. She made 1,670 mL of orange juice on Tuesday. If she poured the orange juice equally into 6 containers, how much orange juice was there in each container?

Unit 13: BAR GRAPHS

Example:

Mr. Ford sells technology products in his store. He recorded the sales of these products for the month of February in the bar graph below. Study the bar graph carefully and answer the questions.

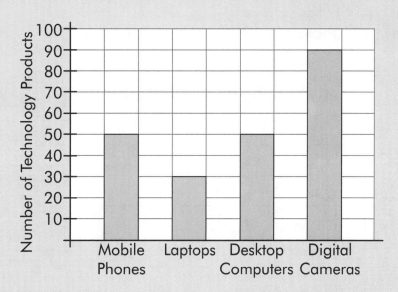

Technology Products Sold in the Month of February

1. How many digital cameras did Mr. Ford sell?   __90__

2. How many laptops did Mr. Ford sell?   __30__

3. How many more desktop computers than laptops did Mr. Ford sell?

    50 − 30 = __20__

4. How many fewer mobile phones than digital cameras did Mr. Ford sell?

    90 − 50 = __40__

5. How many technology products did Mr. Ford sell altogether in the month of February?

    50 + 30 + 50 + 90 = __220__

1. The picture graph below shows the favorite colors of a class of 40 students.

blue	☆ ☆ ☆ ☆ ☆ ☆ ☆ ☆ ☆ ☆ ☆
green	☆ ☆ ☆ ☆ ☆
purple	☆ ☆ ☆ ☆ ☆ ☆ ☆ ☆
red	☆ ☆ ☆ ☆ ☆ ☆ ☆
yellow	☆ ☆ ☆ ☆ ☆
	Each ☆ stands for 1 student.

Use the information above to complete the bar graph.

Favorite Colors of the Students

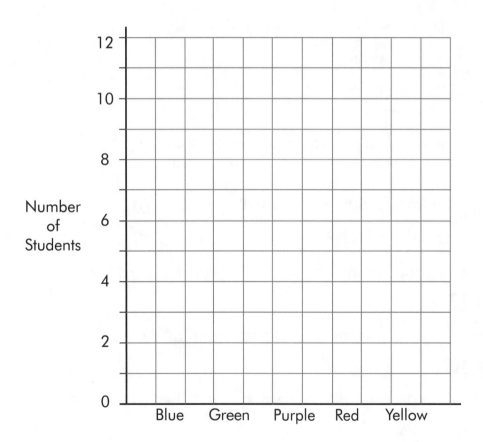

2. The picture graph below shows the number of adults at different booths during a travel exhibition.

China	☆ ☆ ☆ ☆ ☆ ☆ ☆
Europe	☆ ☆ ☆ ☆ ☆ ☆ ☆ ☆ ☆ ☆ ☆ ☆ ☆
Japan	☆ ☆ ☆ ☆ ☆ ☆ ☆ ☆ ☆ ☆
Australia	☆ ☆ ☆ ☆ ☆
Saudi Arabia	☆ ☆ ☆ ☆ ☆ ☆ ☆ ☆
Each ☆ stands for 1 adult.	

Use the information above to complete the bar graph.

Number of Adults at Different Booths

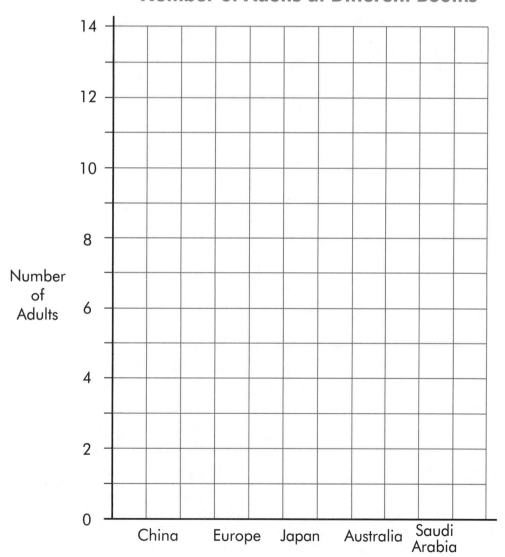

Singapore Math Level 3A & 3B

3. Justin and his friends played a board game. The points scored by the four boys are shown below.

Akmed	Luke	Justin	Brad
95	80	75	65

Use the information above to complete the bar graph.

Points Scored

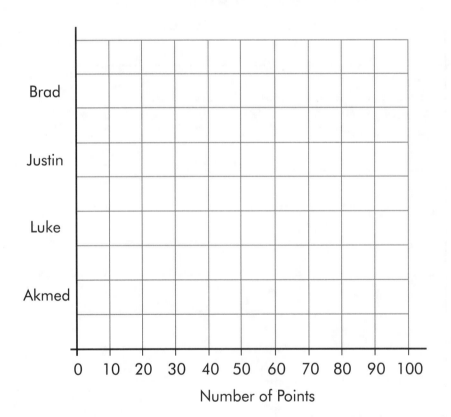

Singapore Math Level 3A & 3B

4. Mrs. Jones works at a dry cleaners. The number of pieces of laundry cleaned in a day is shown below.

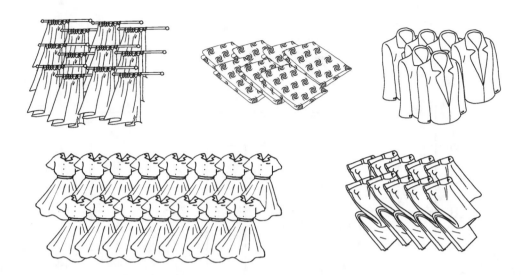

Use the information to complete the bar graph.

Items Cleaned at the Dry Cleaners

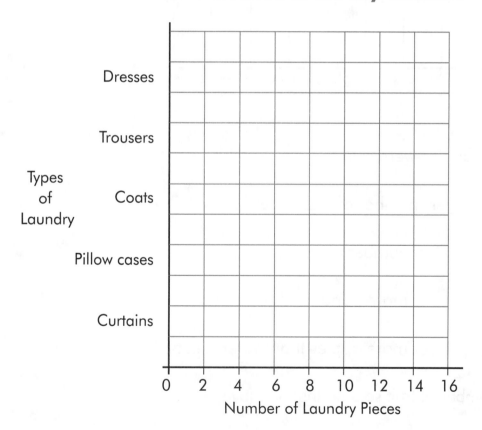

Singapore Math Level 3A & 3B

5. A fruit seller sold some fruit on Sunday. He recorded the number of pieces he sold in the bar graph below. Study the bar graph carefully and fill in each blank with the correct answer.

Fruit Sold on Sunday

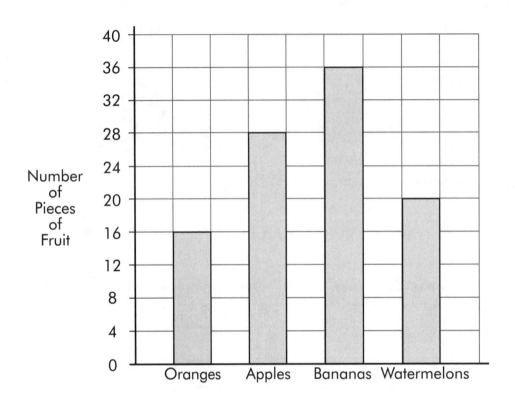

(a) _____ apples were sold.

(b) He sold the largest number of _____.

(c) He sold the smallest number of _____.

(d) He sold _____ more bananas than oranges.

(e) He sold _____ more apples than watermelons.

(f) The total number of fruit sold on that Sunday was _____.

Singapore Math Level 3A & 3B

6. Ana and her sister went to a park. They drew a bar graph of what they saw at the park. Study the bar graph carefully and fill in each blank with the correct answer.

Animals at a Park

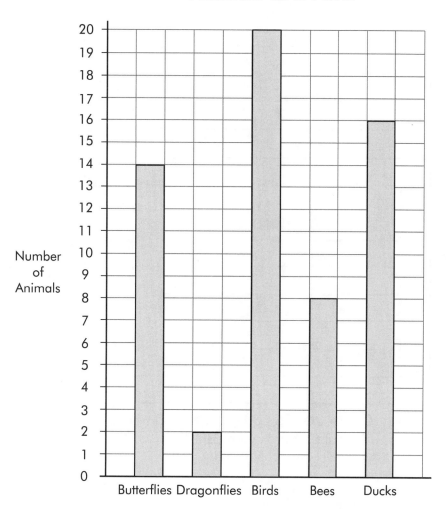

(a) They saw _____ birds.

(b) There were _____ more ducks than butterflies.

(c) There were _____ fewer bees than birds.

(d) They saw the least number of _____.

(e) They saw the most number of _____.

(f) They saw _____ animals altogether at the park.

7. Jorge saved some money in a week. He recorded the amount of money he saved in the bar graph below. Study the bar graph carefully and fill in each blank with the correct answer.

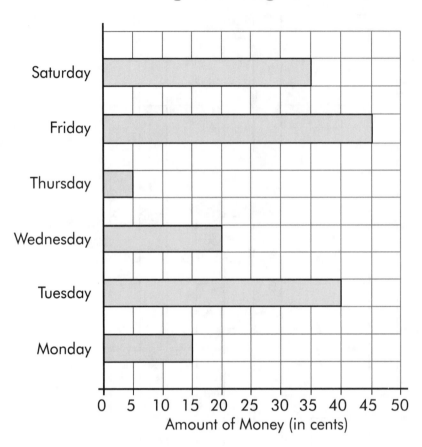

Jorge's Savings in a Week

Amount of Money (in cents)

(a) He saved _____ cents on Friday.

(b) He saved _____ cents more on Tuesday than on Monday.

(c) He saved 7 times more on Saturday than on _____.

(d) He saved $_____ altogether in a week.

(e) Jorge needs $10 to buy a present for his mother.

He needs to save $_____ more.

Singapore Math Level 3A & 3B

8. The bar graph below illustrates the different types of instruments played by the students in a music school. Study the bar graph carefully and fill in each blank with the correct answer.

Instruments Played in a Music School

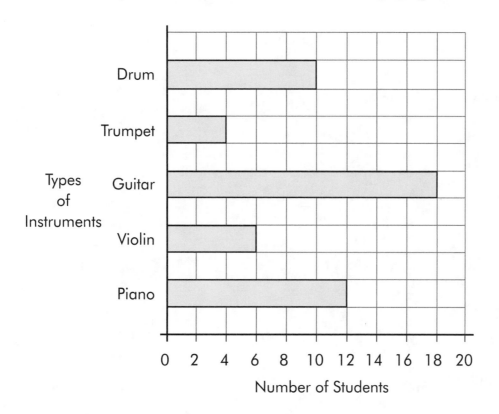

(a) _____ students play violin.

(b) _____ students play drum.

(c) _____ more students play guitar than trumpet.

(d) _____ fewer students play piano than guitar.

(e) There are _____ students in the music school.

Singapore Math Level 3A & 3B

Unit 14: FRACTIONS

Examples:

1. Find the equivalent fractions.

$$\frac{2}{3} = \frac{\boxed{6}}{9} = \frac{8}{\boxed{12}}$$

$$\frac{2 \times 3}{3 \times 3} = \frac{6}{9}$$

$$\frac{2 \times 4}{3 \times 4} = \frac{8}{12}$$

2. Which fraction is smaller, $\frac{5}{6}$ or $\frac{3}{12}$?

$$\frac{5 \times 2}{6 \times 2} = \frac{10}{12}$$

The smaller fraction is $\underline{\frac{3}{12}}$.

3. Add $\frac{1}{8}$ and $\frac{1}{4}$.

$$\frac{1 \times 2}{4 \times 2} = \frac{2}{8}$$

$$\frac{1}{8} + \frac{2}{8} = \underline{\frac{3}{8}}$$

4. What is $1 - \frac{2}{9} - \frac{2}{3}$?

$$1 = \frac{9}{9}$$

$$\frac{2 \times 3}{3 \times 3} = \frac{6}{9}$$

$$\frac{9}{9} - \frac{2}{9} - \frac{6}{9} = \underline{\frac{1}{9}}$$

Singapore Math Level 3A & 3B

Study the following diagrams. Fill in each box with the correct answer.

1.

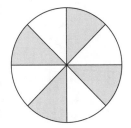

$$\frac{4}{\boxed{}}$$

2.

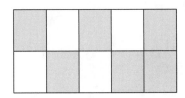

$$\frac{6}{\boxed{}}$$

3.

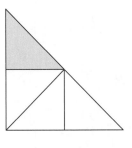

$$\frac{\boxed{}}{4}$$

4.

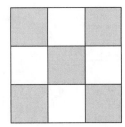

$$\frac{\boxed{}}{9}$$

5.

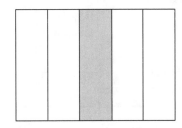

$$\frac{1}{\boxed{}}$$

Singapore Math Level 3A & 3B

Shade the correct parts to show the equivalent fraction. Write the equivalent fraction in the boxes provided.

6.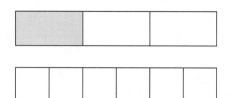

$$\frac{1}{3} = \frac{\square}{\square}$$

7.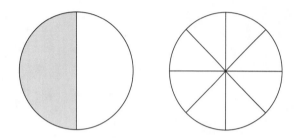

$$\frac{1}{2} = \frac{\square}{\square}$$

8.

$$\frac{3}{4} = \frac{\square}{\square}$$

9.

$$\frac{4}{6} = \frac{\square}{\square}$$

10.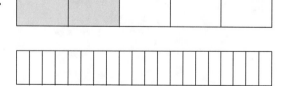

$$\frac{2}{5} = \frac{\square}{\square}$$

Singapore Math Level 3A & 3B

Fill in each box with the correct answer to make the equivalent fraction.

11. $\dfrac{2}{3} = \dfrac{\boxed{}}{9}$

12. $\dfrac{4}{8} = \dfrac{20}{\boxed{}}$

13. $\dfrac{3}{7} = \dfrac{\boxed{}}{28}$

14. $\dfrac{1}{10} = \dfrac{8}{\boxed{}}$

15. $\dfrac{5}{9} = \dfrac{35}{\boxed{}}$

16. $\dfrac{3}{4} = \dfrac{12}{\boxed{}}$

17. $\dfrac{7}{12} = \dfrac{\boxed{}}{36}$

18. $\dfrac{2}{6} = \dfrac{\boxed{}}{36}$

19. $\dfrac{6}{11} = \dfrac{42}{\boxed{}}$

20. $\dfrac{3}{5} = \dfrac{\boxed{}}{30}$

List all of the equivalent fractions.

21. $\dfrac{1}{5} = \dfrac{\boxed{}}{10} = \dfrac{3}{\boxed{}} = \dfrac{4}{\boxed{}} = \dfrac{5}{\boxed{}}$

22. $\dfrac{3}{8} = \dfrac{\boxed{}}{16} = \dfrac{\boxed{}}{24} = \dfrac{12}{\boxed{}} = \dfrac{15}{\boxed{}}$

23. $\dfrac{2}{5} = \dfrac{4}{\boxed{}} = \dfrac{\boxed{}}{15} = \dfrac{8}{\boxed{}} = \dfrac{10}{\boxed{}}$

24. $\dfrac{1}{4} = \dfrac{2}{\boxed{}} = \dfrac{\boxed{}}{12} = \dfrac{4}{\boxed{}} = \dfrac{5}{\boxed{}}$

Singapore Math Level 3A & 3B

25. $\dfrac{1}{7} = \dfrac{\Box}{14} = \dfrac{\Box}{21} = \dfrac{4}{\Box} = \dfrac{5}{\Box}$

Write each fraction in its simplest form.

26. $\dfrac{7}{21} = \dfrac{\Box}{\Box}$

27. $\dfrac{3}{9} = \dfrac{\Box}{\Box}$

28. $\dfrac{8}{16} = \dfrac{\Box}{\Box}$

29. $\dfrac{36}{45} = \dfrac{\Box}{\Box}$

30. $\dfrac{35}{42} = \dfrac{\Box}{\Box}$

31. $\dfrac{9}{63} = \dfrac{\Box}{\Box}$

32. $\dfrac{44}{66} = \dfrac{\Box}{\Box}$

33. $\dfrac{64}{72} = \dfrac{\Box}{\Box}$

34. $\dfrac{12}{18} = \dfrac{\Box}{\Box}$

35. $\dfrac{9}{24} = \dfrac{\Box}{\Box}$

Fill in each blank with the correct fraction.

36.

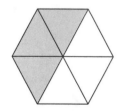 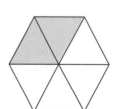

_____ is greater than _____.

37.

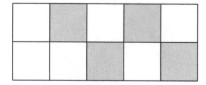 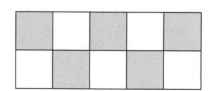

_____ is smaller than _____.

168

Singapore Math Level 3A & 3B

38.

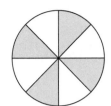

_____ is smaller than _____.

39.

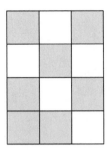 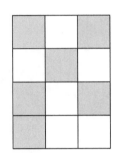

_____ is greater than _____.

40.

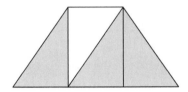

_____ is greater than _____.

Compare these fractions. Circle the smaller fraction.

41. $\dfrac{1}{6}$ and $\dfrac{5}{6}$

42. $\dfrac{4}{9}$ and $\dfrac{2}{9}$

43. $\dfrac{3}{6}$ and $\dfrac{3}{9}$

44. $\dfrac{5}{8}$ and $\dfrac{5}{11}$

45. $\dfrac{7}{12}$ and $\dfrac{7}{9}$

Singapore Math Level 3A & 3B

Compare these fractions. Circle the larger fraction.

46. $\frac{2}{3}$ and $\frac{6}{12}$

47. $\frac{3}{8}$ and $\frac{2}{5}$

48. $\frac{4}{6}$ and $\frac{2}{8}$

49. $\frac{2}{7}$ and $\frac{1}{9}$

50. $\frac{3}{11}$ and $\frac{1}{4}$

Arrange the fractions in order. Begin with the largest.

51. $\frac{3}{9}$, $\frac{8}{9}$, $\frac{5}{9}$ _____

52. $\frac{4}{6}$, $\frac{2}{8}$, $\frac{3}{4}$ _____

53. $\frac{7}{12}$, $\frac{3}{4}$, $\frac{1}{6}$ _____

54. $\frac{2}{5}$, $\frac{8}{9}$, $\frac{4}{15}$ _____

55. $\frac{6}{7}$, $\frac{6}{12}$, $\frac{6}{9}$ _____

Arrange the fractions in order. Begin with the smallest.

56. $\frac{2}{3}$, $\frac{2}{5}$, $\frac{2}{4}$ _____

57. $\frac{3}{8}$, $\frac{4}{6}$, $\frac{1}{4}$ _____

58. $\frac{6}{10}$, $\frac{3}{6}$, $\frac{1}{5}$ _____

Singapore Math Level 3A & 3B

59. $\dfrac{12}{20}, \ \dfrac{18}{20}, \ \dfrac{11}{20}$ _____

60. $\dfrac{4}{7}, \ \dfrac{5}{6}, \ \dfrac{2}{3}$ _____

Add these fractions.

61. $\dfrac{2}{3} + \dfrac{1}{9} =$

62. $\dfrac{1}{4} + \dfrac{1}{2} =$

63. $\dfrac{5}{12} + \dfrac{1}{6} =$

64. $\dfrac{2}{5} + \dfrac{3}{10} =$

65. $\dfrac{3}{8} + \dfrac{1}{4} =$

Subtract these fractions.

66. $\dfrac{1}{2} - \dfrac{1}{5} =$

67. $\dfrac{4}{5} - \dfrac{7}{10} =$

68. $\dfrac{7}{8} - \dfrac{3}{4} =$

69. $\dfrac{5}{6} - \dfrac{5}{12} =$

70. $\dfrac{4}{9} - \dfrac{1}{3} =$

Singapore Math Level 3A & 3B

Solve the problems below. Write the correct answers on the lines.

71. Find the sum of $\frac{1}{9}$, $\frac{1}{3}$, and $\frac{4}{9}$.

72. Find the sum of $\frac{1}{4}$, $\frac{3}{8}$, and $\frac{1}{8}$.

73. Find $1 - \frac{7}{12} - \frac{1}{6}$.

74. Find $1 - \frac{1}{3} - \frac{5}{9}$. _____

75. What is $\frac{3}{10} + \frac{1}{2} + \frac{1}{10}$? _____

76. What is $\frac{2}{6} + \frac{1}{3} + \frac{1}{6}$? _____

77. What is $1 - \frac{3}{8} - \frac{1}{2}$? _____

78. What is $1 - \frac{3}{5} - \frac{1}{10}$? _____

Singapore Math Level 3A & 3B

Unit 15: TIME

Examples:

1.

11:30

or

30 minutes after 11

2.

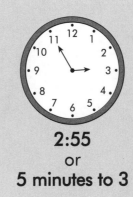

2:55

or

5 minutes to 3

3. 3 hr. 15 min. + 5 hr. 40 min. = <u>**8 hr. 55 min**</u>.

15 min. + 40 min. = 55 min.

3 hr. + 5 hr. = 8 hr.

4. 7 hr. 5 min. – 1 hr. 30 min. = <u>**5 hr. 35 min**</u>.

7 hr. 5 min. = 6 hr. 60 min. + 5 min. = 6 hr. 65 min.

65 min. – 30 min. = 35 min.

6 hr. – 1 hr. = 5 hr.

5. Jessica starts studying for her spelling test at 5:20 P.M.
    She finishes at 6:30 P.M. How long does she study for her spelling test?

1 hr.	10 min.

5:20 P.M.   6:20 P.M. 6:30 P.M.

She studies <u>**1 hr. 10 min.**</u> for her spelling test.

173

Fill in each blank with the correct time.

1.

_____

or

_____

2.

_____

or

_____

3.

_____

or

_____

4.

_____

or

_____

5.

_____

or

_____

6.

_____

or

_____

Singapore Math Level 3A & 3B

7.

_____

or

_____

Fill in each blank with the correct answer.

8. 12:25 is _____ minutes after 12.

9. 8:19 is _____ minutes after 8.

10. 4:10 is 10 minutes after _____.

11. 7:06 is 6 minutes after _____.

12. 3:55 is _____ minutes to 4.

13. 10:38 is _____ minutes to 11.

14. 5:48 is 12 minutes to _____.

15. 9:50 is 10 minutes to _____.

State the following in minutes.

16. 3 hr. = _____ min.

17. 1 hr. 20 min. = _____ min.

18. 4 hr. 5 min. = _____ min.

19. 8 hr. 15 min. = _____ min.

20. 6 hr. 30 min. = _____ min.

Singapore Math Level 3A & 3B

State the following in hours.

21. 420 min. = _____ hr.

22. 300 min. = _____ hr.

23. 600 min. = _____ hr.

24. 240 min. = _____ hr.

25. 540 min. = _____ hr.

State the following in hours and minutes.

26. 75 min. = ____ hr. ____ min.

27. 515 min. = ____ hr. ____ min.

28. 455 min. = ____ hr. ____ min.

29. 190 min. = ____ hr. ____ min.

30. 430 min. = ____ hr. ____ min.

Fill in each blank with the correct answer.

31. 3 hr. 5 min. + 2 hr. 45 min. = ____ hr. ____ min.

32. 7 hr. 17 min. + 3 hr. 38 min. = ____ hr. ____ min.

33. 2 hr. 19 min. + 1 hr. 39 min. = ____ hr. ____ min.

34. 5 hr. 13 min. + 2 hr. 56 min. = ____ hr. ____ min.

35. 6 hr. 28 min. + 4 hr. 50 min. = ____ hr. ____ min.

36. 8 hr. 35 min. + 1 hr. 45 min. = ____ hr. ____ min.

37. 4 hr. 50 min. – 2 hr. 30 min. = ____ hr. ____ min.

38. 10 hr. 35 min. – 7 hr. 25 min. = ____ hr. ____ min.

39. 6 hr. 30 min. – 1 hr. 5 min. = ____ hr. ____ min.

40. 8 hr. 25 min. – 3 hr. 40 min. = ____ hr. ____ min.

41. 5 hr. 15 min. – 1 hr. 45 min. = ____ hr. ____ min.

Singapore Math Level 3A & 3B

42. 10 hr. 20 min. – 4 hr. 50 min. = _____ hr. _____ min.

Draw timelines to find the length of time elapsed.

43. 4:20 P.M. to 4:50 P.M. = _____ minutes

44. 2:30 P.M. to 4:45 P.M. = _____ hours _____ minutes

45. 10:25 A.M. to 1:40 P.M. = _____ hours _____ minutes

46. 11:40 A.M. to 3:35 P.M. = _____ hours _____ minutes

47. 7:10 P.M. to 10:55 P.M. = _____ hours _____ minutes

48. 11:30 A.M. to 7:30 P.M. = _____ hours

49. 1:15 P.M. to 5:55 P.M. = _____ hours _____ minutes

Singapore Math Level 3A & 3B

Draw the correct time on the face of each clock, and write the correct time on the lines provided.

50.

7:00 A.M.

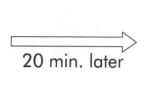 20 min. later

_____

51.

9:30 P.M.

2 hr. 40 min. later

_____

52.

11:15 P.M.

3 hr. 55 min. later

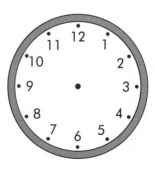

_____

Singapore Math Level 3A & 3B

53.

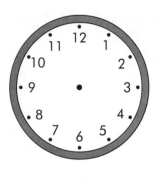 ← 1 hr. 15 min. before

5:30 P.M.

_____

54.

 ← 5 hr. 30 min. before

6:00 A.M.

_____

Solve the following story problems. Show your work in the space below.

55. Shannon and her friends watched a movie. The movie started at 5:30 P.M., and it lasted 1 hr. 20 min. What time did the movie end?

56. John reached his friend's house at 10:15 A.M. He stayed there until 2:55 P.M. How long did he stay at his friend's house?

57. Melissa is meeting her friends for dinner at 7 P.M. It takes 55 minutes to get to the restaurant. At what time should she leave her house if she wants to reach the restaurant on time?

58. Matt is a music teacher. He charges $125 an hour. The table below shows the number of hours he teaches each week. How much does Matt earn in a week?

Days	Number of hours
Monday	3 hr.
Tuesday	2 hr.
Wednesday	3 hr.
Thursday	4 hr.
Friday	2 hr.
Saturday	5 hr.

Singapore Math Level 3A & 3B

59. Grace works at a factory. She is paid $9 per hour. She works 8 hours every day.

   (a) If she works from Monday to Friday, find the total number of hours she works in a week.

   (b) How much does she earn in a week?

60. Dave is a part-time proofreader. He needs 2 hours to proofread a chapter. He is paid $15 for an hour.

   (a) How many hours does he need to proofread six chapters?

   (b) What is the total amount of money he will be paid for proofreading the six chapters?

Singapore Math Level 3A & 3B

REVIEW 6

1. The bar graph shows the favorite fruit of the students in Mrs. William's class. Study the bar graph carefully, and fill in each blank with the correct answer.

Favorite Fruit of Mrs. William's Class

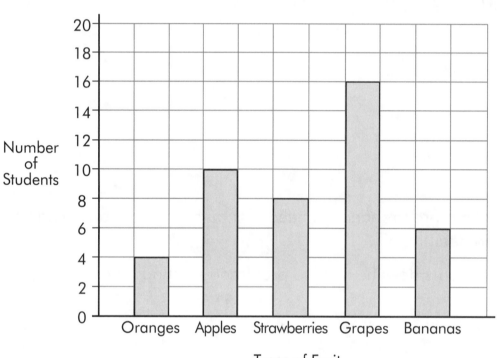

(a) _____ students like strawberries.

(b) _____ students like bananas.

(c) There are _____ more students who like grapes than apples.

(d) There are _____ fewer students who like oranges than bananas.

(e) There are _____ students in the class altogether.

Singapore Math Level 3A & 3B

Fill in each blank to make the fractions equivalent.

2. $\dfrac{2}{9} = \dfrac{\boxed{}}{45}$

3. $\dfrac{3}{7} = \dfrac{12}{\boxed{}}$

Write each fraction in its simplest form.

4. $\dfrac{8}{10} = \dfrac{\boxed{}}{\boxed{}}$

5. $\dfrac{15}{25} = \dfrac{\boxed{}}{\boxed{}}$

Fill in each blank with the correct answer.

6. 76 min. = _____ hr. _____ min.

7. 4 hr. 15 min. = _____ min.

Solve each of the following problems.

8. $\dfrac{1}{4} + \dfrac{2}{8} + \dfrac{3}{8} =$

9. $1 - \dfrac{1}{5} - \dfrac{7}{10} =$

Singapore Math Level 3A & 3B

10. Circle the larger fraction.

(a) $\frac{4}{5}$ and $\frac{3}{10}$ (b) $\frac{8}{9}$ and $\frac{2}{3}$

11. Circle the smaller fraction.

(a) $\frac{2}{3}$ and $\frac{2}{7}$ (b) $\frac{3}{8}$ and $\frac{1}{4}$

12. Arrange the fractions in order. Begin with the largest.

$\frac{2}{3}, \frac{1}{6}, \frac{3}{6}$ _____

13. Arrange the fractions in order. Begin with the smallest.

$\frac{1}{3}, \frac{1}{5}, \frac{1}{9}$ _____

Fill in each blank with the correct answer.

14.

_____ to _____

15. 4 hr. 35 min. + 3 hr. 30 min. = ____ hr. ____ min.

Singapore Math Level 3A & 3B

16. Consuela had just received her test scores. Her scores for the four tests are shown in the table below.

English	Math	Science	Social Studies
95	80	75	80

(a) Use the information above to complete the bar graph.

Consuela's Test Scores

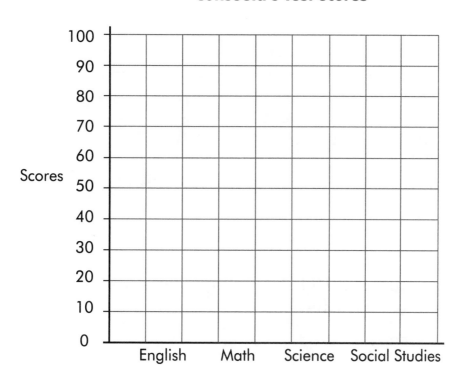

(b) Consuela scored the lowest in _____.

(c) Consuela scored _____ points more in math than in science.

(d) Consuela scored _____ points less in social studies than in English.

Fill in each blank with the correct answer.

17. 9 hr. 15 min. – 3 hr. 45 min. = ____ hr. ____ min.

Singapore Math Level 3A & 3B

Draw the correct time on the face of each clock.

18.

30 min. before

10:10 P.M.

19.

3:20 P.M.

4 hr. 20 min. later

20. Maggie went to the library at 3:15 P.M. She stayed there for 2 hr. 25 min. Draw a timeline to find the time she left the library.

Singapore Math Level 3A & 3B

Unit 16: ANGLES

Examples:

1. Identify the right angle in the triangle below.

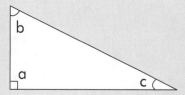

   Angle **a** is the right angle.

2. Arrange the angles in order. Begin with the smallest.

   p, r, q

3. How many sides and angles are there in the shape below?

   There are **8** sides and **8** angles in the shape.

Singapore Math Level 3A & 3B

1. Amit arranges some toothpicks as shown below. Circle the arrangements that form an angle.

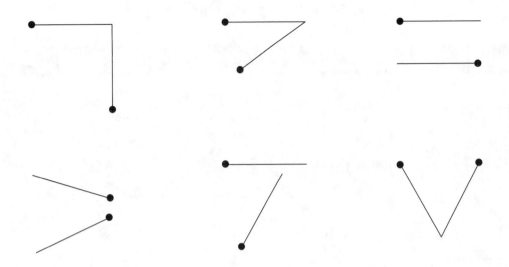

Circle the larger angle for each pair.

2.

3.

4.

Singapore Math Level 3A & 3B

5.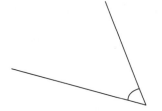

6.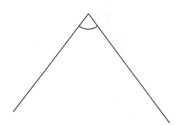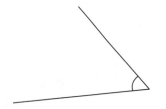

Circle the smaller angle for each pair.

7.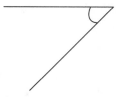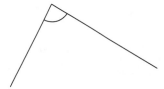

8.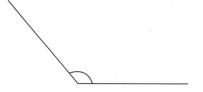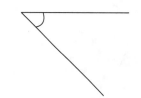

9.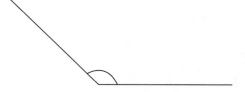

Singapore Math Level 3A & 3B

10.

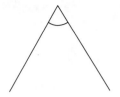 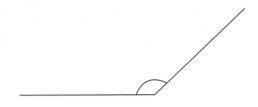

11.

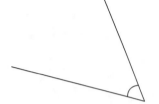 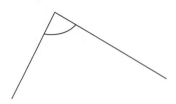

Mark one angle in each shape.

12.

13.

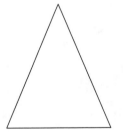

14.

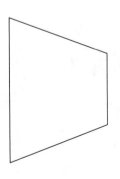

15.

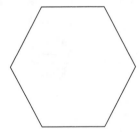

16.

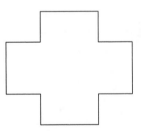

Singapore Math Level 3A & 3B

Mark one angle in each object.

17.

20.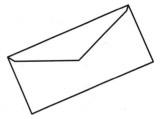

18.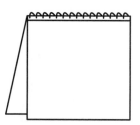

21.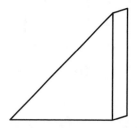

19.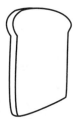

Fill in each blank with the correct answer.

22.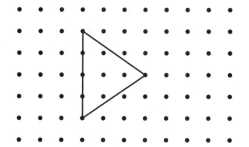

This figure has _____ sides and _____ angles.

23.

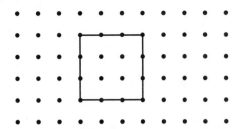

This figure has _____ sides and _____ angles.

24.

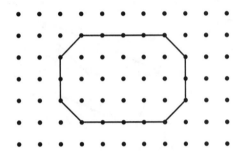

This figure has _____ sides and _____ angles.

25.

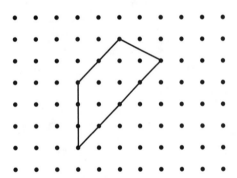

This figure has _____ sides and _____ angles.

26.

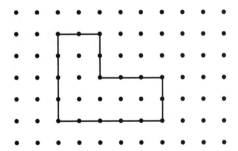

This figure has _____ sides and _____ angles.

Singapore Math Level 3A & 3B

Mark all the right angles in each figure.

27.

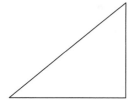

28.

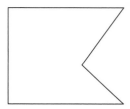

29.

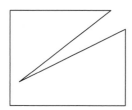

30.

31.

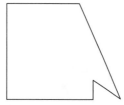

32. Study the following angles carefully. Fill in each blank with the correct answer.

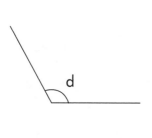 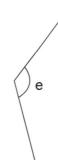 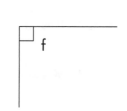

(a) Which angles are smaller than a right angle? _____

(b) Which angles are larger than a right angle? _____

(c) Which angles are right angles? _____

Singapore Math Level 3A & 3B

33. Study the following angles carefully. Fill in each blank with the correct answer.

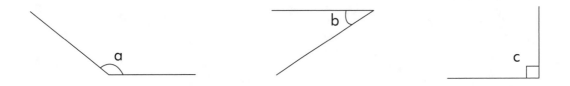

(a) Angle _____ is the smallest.

(b) Angle _____ is the largest.

(c) Angle _____ is larger than angle c.

(d) Arrange the angles in order. Begin with the largest angle.

_____, _____, _____

34.

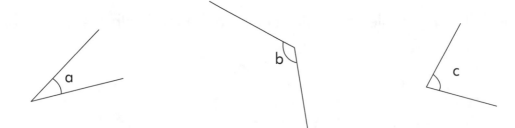

(a) Angle _____ is the largest.

(b) Angle _____ is the smallest.

(c) Angle _____ is smaller than angle c.

(d) Arrange the angles in order. Begin with the smallest angle.

_____, _____, _____

Singapore Math Level 3A & 3B

Fill in each blank with the correct answer.

35.

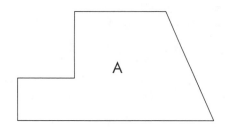

Figure A has _____ sides and _____ right angles.

36.

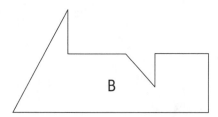

Figure B has _____ sides and _____ right angles.

37.

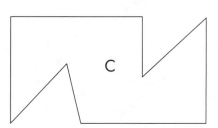

Figure C has _____ sides and _____ right angles.

38.

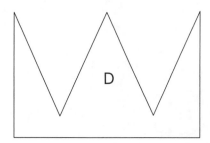

Figure D has _____ sides and _____ right angles.

Singapore Math Level 3A & 3B

Unit 17: PERPENDICULAR AND PARALLEL LINES

Examples:

1. Is AB perpendicular to (⊥) CD?

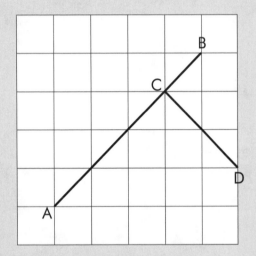

Yes, AB is perpendicular to (⊥) CD.

2. Identify all parallel lines.

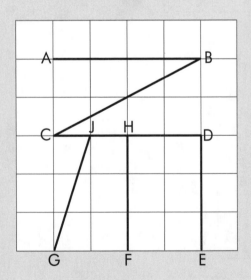

AB is parallel to (//) CD.
DE is parallel to (//) HF.

Singapore Math Level 3A & 3B

Put a check mark (✓) in the box if the pair of lines is perpendicular. Put an X if the pair of lines is not perpendicular.

1.

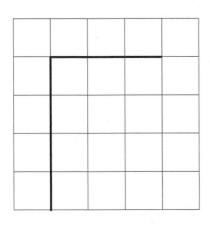

4.

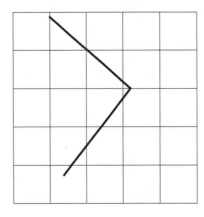

2.

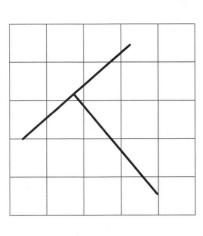

5.

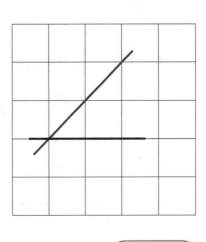

3.

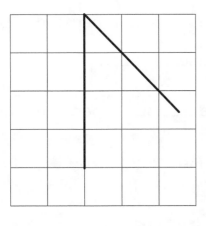

Fill in each blank with the correct answer.

6.

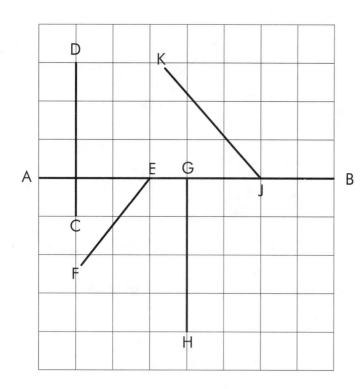

Line _____ is perpendicular

to Line _____.

Line _____ is perpendicular

to Line _____.

7.

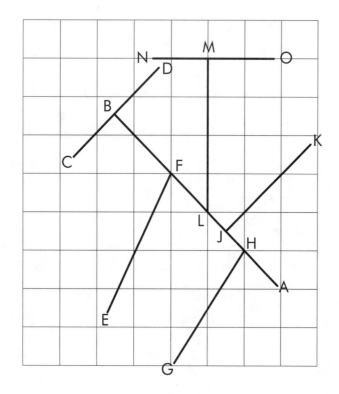

Line _____ is perpendicular

to Line _____.

Line _____ is perpendicular

to Line _____.

Line _____ is perpendicular

to Line _____.

Singapore Math Level 3A & 3B

For each figure, identify all pairs of perpendicular lines.

8.

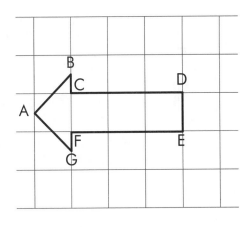

9.

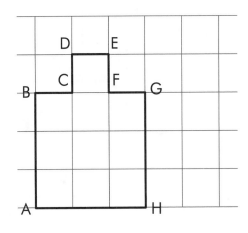

_____   _____

Draw 3 lines perpendicular to YZ. Each line must pass through at least two points on the grid.

10.

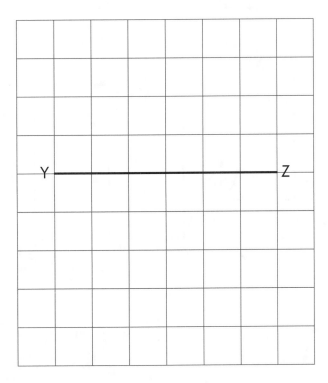

199

11.

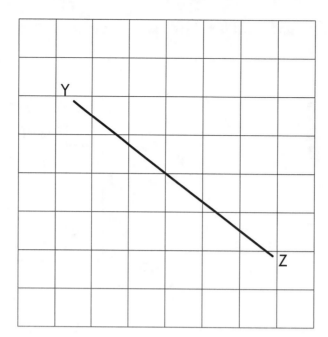

12.

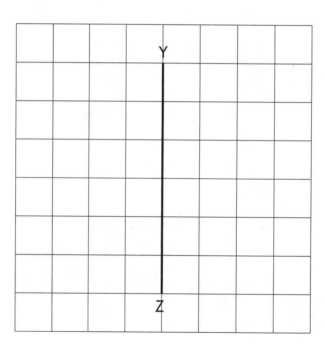

Put a check mark (✓) in the box if the pair of lines is parallel. Put an X if the pair of lines is not parallel.

13.

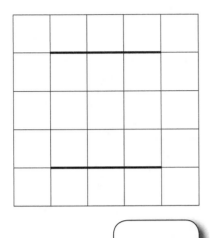

16.

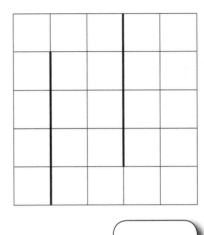

14.

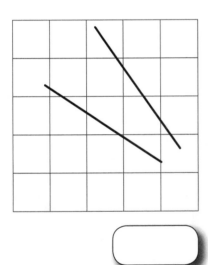

17.

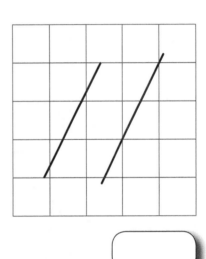

15.

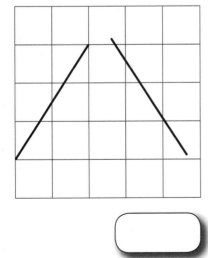

For each figure, identify the pairs of parallel lines.

18.

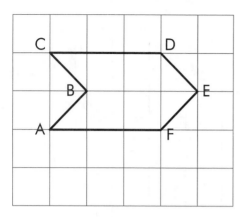

_____

19.

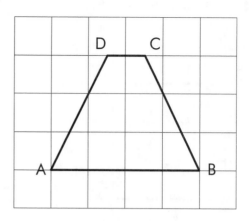

_____

Fill in each blank with the correct answer.

20.

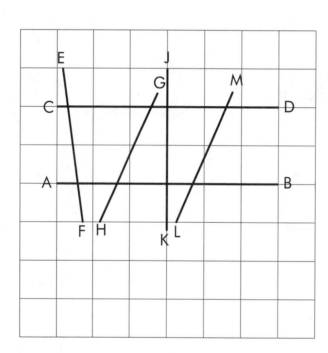

Line _____ is parallel to Line _____.

Line _____ is parallel to Line _____.

Singapore Math Level 3A & 3B

21.

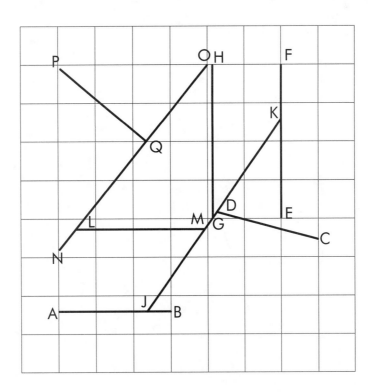

Line _____ is parallel to Line _____.

Line _____ is parallel to Line _____.

Line _____ is parallel to Line _____.

Draw 2 lines parallel to YZ. Each line must pass through at least two points on the grid.

22.

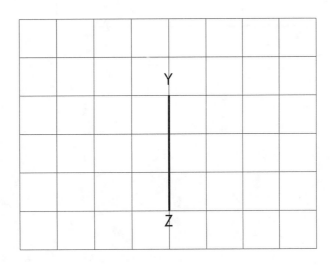

Singapore Math Level 3A & 3B

23.

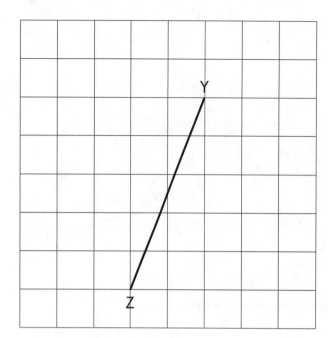

24.

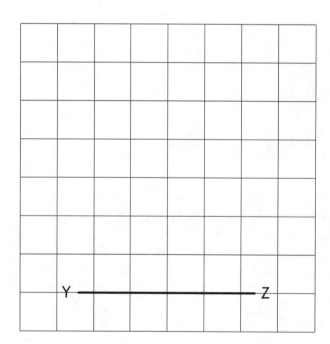

Unit 18: AREA AND PERIMETER

Examples:

1. Find the area of the figure below.

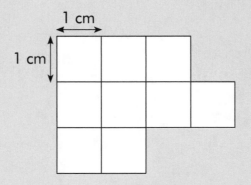

The figure is made up of nine 1-cm squares.

The area of each 1-cm square = $1 \times 1 = 1$ cm².

The area of the figure = 9×1 cm² = **9 cm²**.

2. Find the perimeter of the rectangle below.

15 in.

8 in.

Perimeter = $8 + 15 + 8 + 15$

       = **46 in.**

Singapore Math Level 3A & 3B

Find the area of each figure.

1.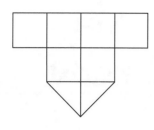

   Area = _____ square units

2.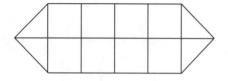

   Area = _____ square units

3.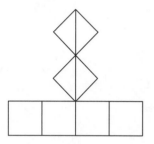

   Area = _____ square units

4.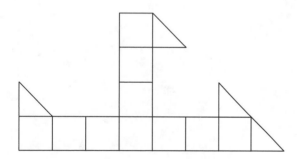

   Area = _____ square units

5.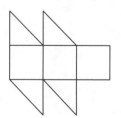

   Area = _____ square units

Singapore Math Level 3A & 3B

6. The area of each square is 1 cm². Find the area of the shaded figures below.

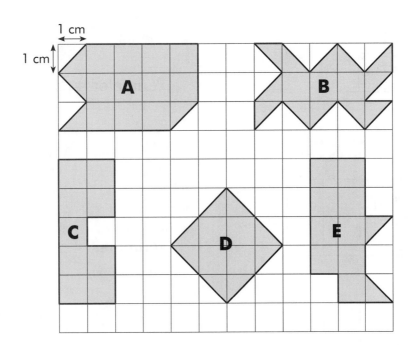

(a) The area of Figure A is _____ cm².

(b) The area of Figure B is _____ cm².

(c) The area of Figure C is _____ cm².

(d) The area of Figure D is _____ cm².

(e) The area of Figure E is _____ cm².

(f) Figures _____ and _____ have the same area.

(g) Figure _____ has the smallest area.

(h) Figure _____ has the largest area.

Singapore Math Level 3A & 3B

Find the perimeter of each shaded figure.

7.

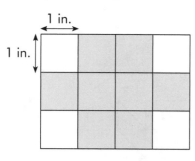

Perimeter = _____ in.

8.

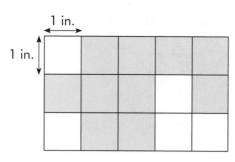

Perimeter = _____ in.

9.

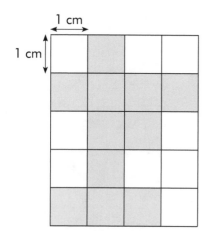

Perimeter = _____ cm

10.

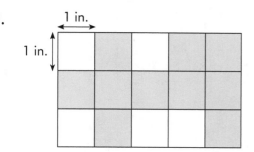

Perimeter = _____ in.

11.

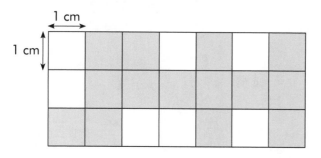

Perimeter = _____ cm

Singapore Math Level 3A & 3B

12. Study the following figures carefully. Fill in each blank with the correct answer.

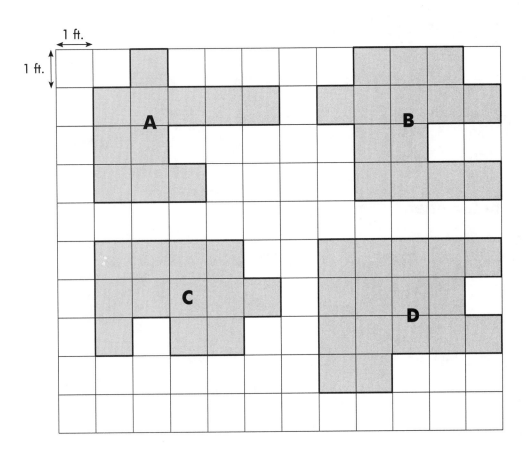

(a) The area of Figure A is _____ ft.².

(b) The area of Figure B is _____ ft.².

(c) The area of Figure C is _____ ft.².

(d) The area of Figure D is _____ ft.².

(e) The perimeter of Figure A is _____ ft.

(f) The perimeter of Figure B is _____ ft.

(g) The perimeter of Figure C is _____ ft.

(h) The perimeter of Figure D is _____ ft.

Singapore Math Level 3A & 3B

(i)   Figure _____ has the largest area.

(j)   Figure _____ has the smallest area.

(k)   Figure _____ has the shortest perimeter.

(l)   Figure _____ has the longest perimeter.

Find the perimeter of each figure.

13.

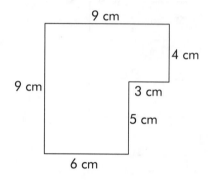

Perimeter = _____ cm

15.

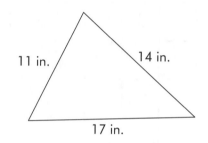

Perimeter = _____ in.

14.

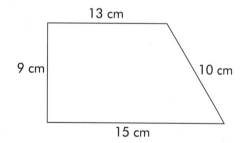

Perimeter = _____ cm

16.

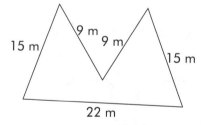

Perimeter = _____ m

Singapore Math Level 3A & 3B

Find the area and perimeter of each figure.

17.

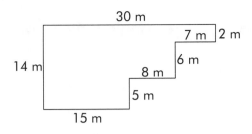

Perimeter = _____ m

20.

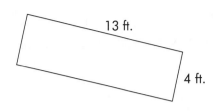

Area = _____ ft.²

Perimeter = _____ ft.

18.

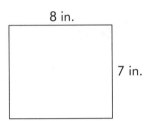

Area = _____ in.²

Perimeter = _____ in.

21.

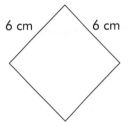

Area = _____ cm²

Perimeter = _____ cm

19.

Area = _____ cm²

Perimeter = _____ cm

22.

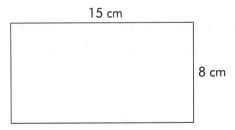

Area = _____ cm²

Perimeter = _____ cm

Singapore Math Level 3A & 3B

Solve the following story problems. Show your work in the space below.

23. Andrew is making a rectangle using a piece of wire. The rectangle is 4 cm by 8 cm. How much wire does Andrew need?

24. Mercy sweeps the kitchen. The kitchen is 6 m by 8 m. How much floor space does Mercy sweep?

25. Justin is jogging along a square field. If he has jogged 240 yd. to complete 1 lap, what is the length of each side of the square field?

Singapore Math Level 3A & 3B

REVIEW 7

1. Mark all angles smaller than a right angle in the figure below.

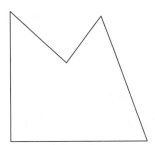

Fill in each blank with the correct answer.

2.

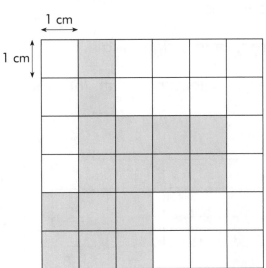

   (a) The area of the above figure is _____ cm².

   (b) The perimeter of the above figure is _____ cm.

3.

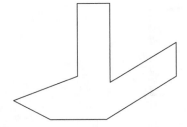

   This figure has _____ sides and _____ right angles.

4. Identify all the perpendicular lines in the figure below.

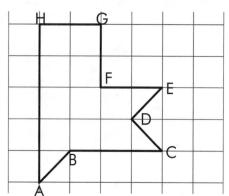

_____

5.

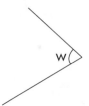 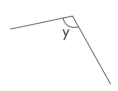

(a) Angle _____ is the smallest.

(b) Angle _____ is the largest.

(c) Angle _____ is larger than a right angle.

(d) Arrange the angles in order. Begin with the smallest angle.

_____, _____, _____, _____

6.

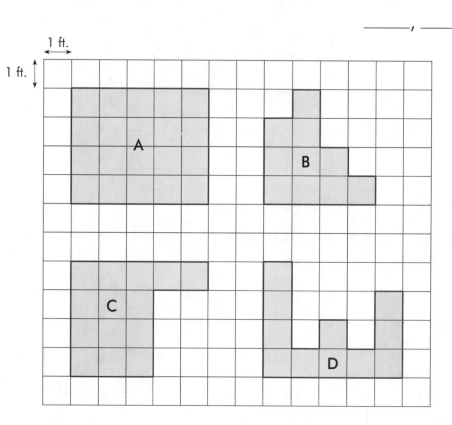

Singapore Math Level 3A & 3B

(a) The area of Figure A is _____ ft.²

(b) The area of Figure B is _____ ft.²

(c) The area of Figure C is _____ ft.²

(d) The area of Figure D is _____ ft.²

(e) The perimeter of Figure A is _____ ft.

(f) The perimeter of Figure B is _____ ft.

(g) The perimeter of Figure C is _____ ft.

(h) The perimeter of Figure D is _____ ft.

(i) Figure _____ has the smallest area.

(j) Figure _____ has the longest perimeter.

7. Identify all the parallel lines in the figure below.

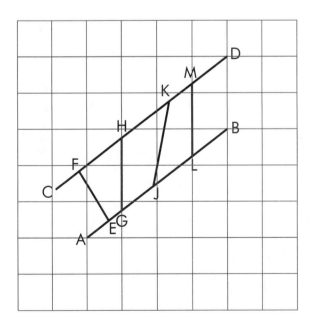

8. Find the perimeter of the figure below.

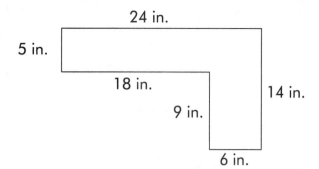

_____

9. Identify two pairs of parallel lines in the figure below.

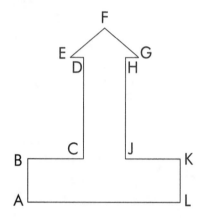

_____

10. Draw 2 lines perpendicular to Line CD. Each line must pass through at least two points on the grid.

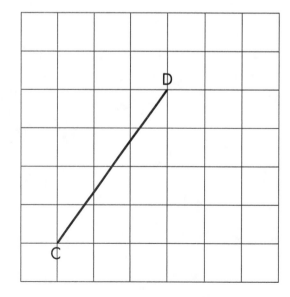

Singapore Math Level 3A & 3B

11. Mark all the right angles in the figure below.

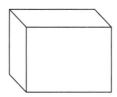

12. Find the area and perimeter of the figure below.

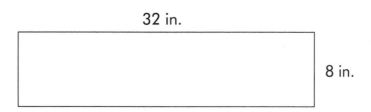

32 in.

8 in.

Area = _____ in.²   Perimeter = _____ in.

13. Find the area of the square.

12 cm

_____

Solve the following story problems. Show your work in the space below.

14. The figure below is made up of four squares. Find the perimeter of the figure.

9 cm

Singapore Math Level 3A & 3B

15. The width of a box is 15 in. Its length is twice its width. What is the perimeter of the box?

16. The figure below shows the floor plan of a room. What is the area of the room?

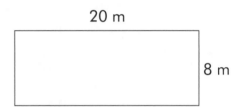

20 m

8 m

17. Emma has a piece of wrapping paper 30 in. by 15 in. She uses 80 in.² of the wrapping paper. What is the area of the remaining wrapping paper?

18. Jennifer uses half of a piece of drawing paper. The remaining drawing paper measures 14 cm by 11 cm. What is the total area of the piece of drawing paper?

19. Becky cuts a rectangle from a piece of cardboard as shown below. What is the perimeter of the remaining cardboard?

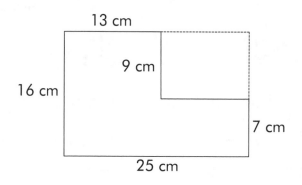

20. Nathan glued two similar rectangular stickers on a piece of paper as shown below. Find the perimeter of the two stickers.

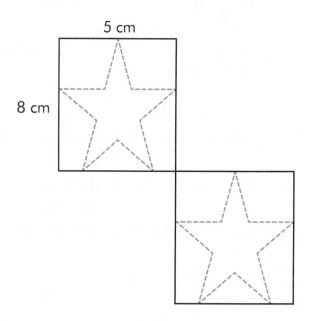

Singapore Math Level 3A & 3B

Fill in each blank with the correct answer.

1.

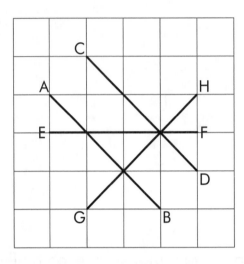

(a) Identify all pairs of perpendicular lines.   _____

(b) Identify all pairs of parallel lines.   _____

2. Sam wants to watch his favorite cartoon show. It starts at 4:45 P.M. The cartoon lasts 45 minutes. The cartoon show will end at _____.

3. Fill in each blank with the correct answer.

(a) 307 cm = ____ m ____ cm

(b) 43 kg 210 g = _____ g

(c) 80 L 10 mL = _____ mL

(d) 4 km 40 m = _____ m

4. The bar graph shows the different types of products sold at a bookstore in a day.

Types of Products Sold at a Bookstore

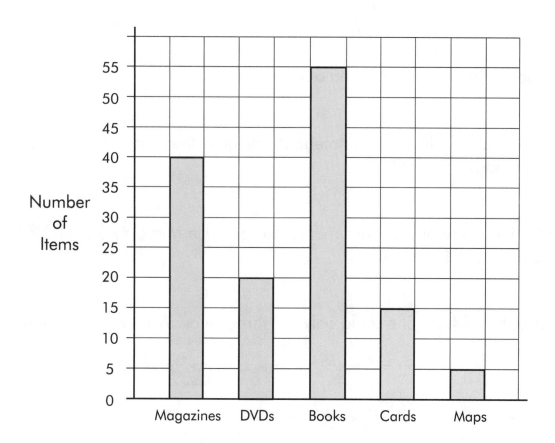

Types of products

(a) The item that sold the most was _____.

(b) _____ magazines were sold.

(c) There were _____ more books sold than cards.

(d) There were _____ fewer maps sold than DVDs.

(e) A total of _____ cards and maps were sold.

5. Below are some items sold in an office supply store.

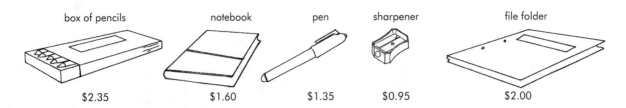

box of pencils	notebook	pen	sharpener	file folder
$2.35	$1.60	$1.35	$0.95	$2.00

(a) Pam bought a box of pencils and a sharpener. How much did she pay altogether?

_____

(b) Felipe bought a folder and a notebook. He gave the cashier $5.00. How much change did he receive?

_____

(c) Austin needed to buy a sharpener and a pen. He had only $2.00. How much more money did he need?

_____

(d) Adriana had $4.00. She could only buy three items. What were the three items?

_____

6. Fill in each box with the correct answer to make the fraction equivalent.

(a) $\dfrac{3}{7} = \dfrac{9}{\square}$

(c) $\dfrac{8}{11} = \dfrac{32}{\square}$

(b) $\dfrac{2}{4} = \dfrac{\square}{16}$

(d) $\dfrac{4}{9} = \dfrac{\square}{27}$

7. Write each fraction in its simplest form.

(a) $\dfrac{8}{12} = \dfrac{\square}{\square}$

(c) $\dfrac{6}{8} = \dfrac{\square}{\square}$

(b) $\dfrac{3}{6} = \dfrac{\square}{\square}$

(d) $\dfrac{4}{10} = \dfrac{\square}{\square}$

Singapore Math Level 3A & 3B

8. Find the area of the shaded figure.

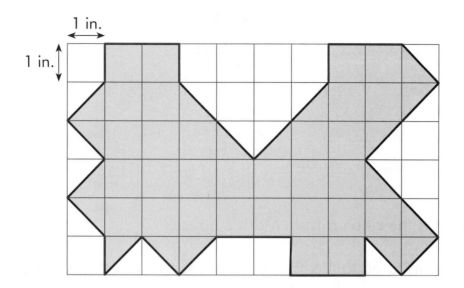

The area of the shaded figure is _____ in.².

9. In the figure below, identify all the angles smaller than a right angle by marking them.

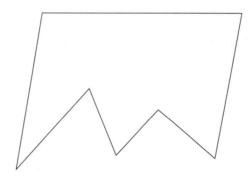

10. Arrange the fractions in order. Begin with the smallest.

$\dfrac{3}{8}$, $\dfrac{3}{4}$, $\dfrac{1}{4}$ _____, _____, _____

11. Study the map below and answer the questions.

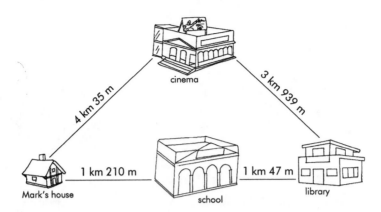

(a) How far is the cinema from Mark's house?   _____ m

(b) Mark wants to go to the library. If he goes to his school first before making his way to the library, what is the total distance that he will travel from his house?

_____ m

(c) If Mark goes to the library by passing the cinema from his house, what is the total distance that he will cover?

_____ km _____ m

(d) Which is a shorter route to the library, by the cinema or by the school?

_____

(e) How much shorter?   _____ km _____ m

Solve the addition problems below.

12. $360.50 + $197.85 = $_____

13. 10 m 36 cm – 2 m 77 cm = _____ m _____ cm

14. 7 km 4 m + 9 km 312 m = _____ km _____ m

15. $469.20 – $87.90 = $_____

16. 63 L 97 mL – 42 L 656 mL = _____ L _____ mL

17. 44 kg 300 g + 29 kg 695 g = _____ kg _____ g

Singapore Math Level 3A & 3B

18. Fill in each blank with *kg* or *g*.

    (a)   The mass of a ruler is 15 _____.

    (b)   The mass of a dictionary is 1 _____.

19.    The time is 1:25 P.M. 30 minutes later, the time will be

    _____.

20. Find the sum of $\frac{1}{9}$ and $\frac{2}{3}$.   _____

Solve the following story problems. Show your work in the space below.

21. Robert is helping to pour a concrete patio. The patio is 12 ft. long and 10 ft. wide. What is the area of the patio?

22. An elephant has a mass of 125 kg 600 g. A lion has a mass of 60 kg 700 g lighter than the elephant. What is the total mass of the two animals?

Singapore Math Level 3A & 3B

23. Marley bought a sofa set and a table. The sofa set cost $3,700, and the table cost $1,900 less than the sofa set. How much did Marley pay for the furniture in all?

24. A ship leaves the port and travels 93 km 650 m to Town B. It then travels to Town C, which is 6 km 770 m away from Town B. How far does the ship travel altogether?

25. Mary cooked 10 L 50 mL of chicken soup on Saturday. She cooked 8 L 960 mL more chicken soup on Sunday than on Saturday. What was the total volume of chicken soup that she had cooked on both days?

CHALLENGE QUESTIONS

Solve the following word problems on another sheet of paper.

1. Mike bought a backpack that cost $29.90. He gave the cashier the exact amount with 7 bills and 4 coins. What were the bills and coins he gave to the cashier?

2. A garden is located exactly halfway between Jamie's house and her school. The distance between the garden and her school is 1 km. What is the distance from Jamie's house to her school?

3. Replace the following letters with digits 1, 2, 3, and 4. The addition of AB and CD is 46. The addition of DC and BA is 64. Find the digits that represent letters A, B, C, and D.

4. Plant A is 1 m tall. Plant B is 50 cm taller than Plant A. Plant C is 5 cm shorter than Plant A. What is the total height of the tallest and the shortest plants?

5. Mr. Robinson flew from Singapore to Tokyo, Japan. The flight lasted 7 hours. Tokyo is an hour ahead of the time in Singapore. If Mr. Robinson reached Tokyo at 7 A.M. on September 14, find the time his flight left Singapore.

6. Grace dropped a string into a measuring cylinder of oil and water. $\frac{1}{4}$ of the string was immersed in oil and water. $\frac{1}{8}$ of the string was immersed in water. If 5 cm of the string was immersed in water, what was the total length of the string?

7. Ken has 3 bills. The first bill is twice the amount of money of the second one. The third bill is ten times the amount of money of the second one. The difference between the largest and the smallest amounts is $45. How much money does Ken have?

Singapore Math Level 3A & 3B

8. It is 12 hours earlier in New York than in Singapore. What will be the time in New York when the clock strikes twelve midnight on Christmas Day in Singapore?

9. Simon's father ate $\frac{1}{2}$ of a pizza. Simon ate $\frac{1}{2}$ of what was left. Simon's mother ate $\frac{1}{2}$ of what was left after Simon had taken his pieces. The remaining 2 pieces of pizza were eaten by Simon's brother. How many pieces of pizza were there at first?

10. Mrs. David bought groceries. She gave the cashier $25. She received the change in 3 bills in two different denominations. One of the bills was 5 times the amount of money of the other bills. The change was between $5 and $10. How much were the groceries?

11. A bean plant grows 1 inch every three days. How tall will the bean plant grow after 30 days?

12. Study the numbers carefully. Find the missing number.

118	159	277
269	?	623
387	513	900

Singapore Math Level 3A & 3B

Unit 1: Numbers 1–10,000

1. **3,625**
2. **9,099**
3. **6,208**
4. **5,817**
5. **8,035**
6. **nine thousand, six hundred ninety-three**
7. **four thousand, three hundred thirteen**
8. **eight thousand, four hundred forty**
9. **seven thousand, fifteen**
10. **six thousand, five hundred five**
11. **8,070, 8,090**
    8,060 – 8,050 = 10
    8,060 + 10 = 8,070
    8,080 + 10 = 8,090
12. **2,211, 2,411**
    2,111 + 100 = 2,211
    2,311 + 100 = 2,411
13. **5,593, 7,593**
    4,593 – 3,593 = 1,000
    4,593 + 1,000 = 5,593
    6,593 + 1,000 = 7,593
14. **2099, 2399**
    2,299 – 2,199 = 100
    1,999 + 100 = 2,099
    2,299 + 100 = 2,399
15. **7,090, 7,110**
    7,080 + 10 = 7,090
    7,100 + 10 = 7,110
16. **3, 7, 4, 0**
17. **9, 3, 6, 1**
18. **7, 0, 0, 1**
19. **6,000, 300, 80, 4**
20. **1,000, 0, 70, 2**
21. **4,000, 900, 50, 1**
22. **800**
23. **2,000**
24. **600**
25. (a) **0**
    (b) **thousands**
    (c) **500**
    (d) **4**
26. (a) **4**
    (b) **ones**
    (c) **20**
    (d) **8**
27. (a) **5**
    (b) **tens**
    (c) **700**

(d) **1**
28. **6,447**
29. **1,047**
30. **4,196**
31. **6,656**
32. **8,942**
33. **3,010**
34. **4,614**
35. **9,999**
36. **5,551**
37. **2,468**
38. **3,829**
39. **2,056**
40. **smaller**
41. **greater**
42. **greater**
43. **greater**
44. **smaller**
45. **1,550, 1,555**
    1,545 – 1,540 = 5
    1,545 + 5 = 1,550
    1,550 + 5 = 1,555
46. **4,769, 4,469**
    4,669 – 4,569 = 100
    4,869 – 100 = 4,769
    4,569 – 100 = 4,469
47. **2,350, 2,370**
    2,340 – 2,330 = 10
    2,340 + 10 = 2,350
    2,360 + 10 = 2,370
48. **7,719, 6,719**
    5,719 – 4,719 = 1,000
    8,719 – 1,000 = 7,719
    7,719 – 1,000 = 6,719
49. **5,896, 5,906**
    5,886 – 5,876 = 10
    5,886 + 10 = 5,896
    5,896 + 10 = 5,906
50. **9,316, 6,193, 3,619, 1,936**
51. **5,850, 5,805, 5,508, 5,058**
52. **9,963, 9,396, 6,939, 3,699**
53. **4,210, 4,120, 2,104, 2,014**
54. **8,616, 8,116, 6,881, 6,818**
55. **1,424, 2,424, 4,424, 8,424**
56. **8,001, 8,011, 8,101, 8,118**
57. **4,025, 4,520, 5,045, 5,240**
58. **3,369, 3,693, 6,339, 6,933**
59. **4,169, 4,619, 4,691, 4,916**
60. **8,621**
61. **3,579**

Unit 2: Adding Numbers up to 10,000

1. 1,386 + 2,001 = **3,387**

```
   1, 3 8 6
 + 2, 0 0 1
   3, 3 8 7
```

2. 5,210 + 4,689 = **9,899**

```
   5, 2 1 0
 + 4, 6 8 9
   9, 8 9 9
```

3. 4,037 + 2,232 = **6,269**

```
   4, 0 3 7
 + 2, 2 3 2
   6, 2 6 9
```

4. 6,512 + 3,076 = **9,588**

```
   6, 5 1 2
 + 3, 0 7 6
   9, 5 8 8
```

5. 4,378 + 1,521 = **5,899**

```
   4, 3 7 8
 + 1, 5 2 1
   5, 8 9 9
```

6. **11, 9**
   1, 1, 9
   3 hundreds 6 tens + 8 hundreds 3 tens
   = 3 + 8 hundreds 6 + 3 tens
   = 11 hundreds 9 tens
   = 1 thousand 1 hundred 9 tens

7. **11, 13, 5**
   1, 2, 3, 5
   5 hundreds 9 tens 3 ones + 6 hundreds 4 tens 2 ones
   = 5 + 6 hundreds 9 + 4 tens 3 + 2 ones
   = 11 hundreds 13 tens 5 ones
   = 1 thousand 2 hundreds 3 tens 5 ones

8. **12, 8, 13**
   1, 2, 9, 3
   7 hundreds 6 tens 9 ones + 5 hundreds 2 tens 4 ones
   = 7 + 5 hundreds 6 + 2 tens 9 + 4 ones
   = 12 hundreds 8 tens 13 ones
   = 1 thousand 2 hundreds 9 tens 3 ones

9. **12, 10, 14**
   1, 3, 1, 4
   4 hundreds 2 tens 5 ones + 8 hundreds 8 tens 9 ones
   = 4 + 8 hundreds 2 + 8 tens 5 + 9 ones
   = 12 hundreds 10 tens 14 ones
   = 1 thousand 3 hundreds 1 ten 4 ones

10. **17, 6, 5**
    1, 7, 6, 5
    9 hundreds 1 ten 5 ones + 8 hundreds 5 tens
    = 9 + 8 hundreds 1 + 5 tens 5 ones
    = 17 hundreds 6 tens 5 ones
    = 1 thousand 7 hundreds 6 tens 5 ones

11. 2,790 + 5,637 = **8,427**

```
   2, 7 9 0
 + 5, 6 3 7
   8, 4 2 7
```

12. 4,078 + 3,659 = **7,737**

```
   4, 0 7 8
 + 3, 6 5 9
   7, 7 3 7
```

13. 8,316 + 1,473 = **9,789**

```
   8, 3 1 6
 + 1, 4 7 3
   9, 7 8 9
```

14.
```
   1, 7 4 5
 + 6, 4 8 7
   8, 2 3 2
```

15.
```
   8, 4 0 0
 + 1, 3 2 4
   9, 7 2 4
```

16.
```
   3, 3 5 6
 + 4, 1 3 4
   7, 4 9 0
```

17.
```
   4, 3 4 8
 + 1, 6 2 5
   5, 9 7 3
```

18.
```
   7, 4 3 0
 + 1, 9 3 2
   9, 3 6 2
```

19.
```
   2, 2 8 2
 + 5, 4 1 3
   7, 6 9 5
```

20.
```
   4, 9 0 8
 + 1, 7 6 7
   6, 6 7 5
```

21.
```
   6, 2 1 0
 + 1, 5 3 8
   7, 7 4 8
```

22.
```
   9, 1 2 6
 +    1 4 2
   9, 2 6 8
```

23.
```
   4, 8 1 3
 + 4, 1 3 5
   8, 9 4 8
```

24.
```
   5, 4 1 0
 + 2, 3 8 5
   7, 7 9 5
```

25.
```
   3, 8 6 9
 + 2, 4 3 5
   6, 3 0 4
```

26.
```
   3, 8 6 3
 + 5, 5 7 6
   9, 4 3 9
```

27.
```
   5, 6 5 7
 + 3, 6 3 8
   9, 2 9 5
```

28.
```
   5, 3 7 5
 + 2, 9 1 7
   8, 2 9 2
```

29.
```
   6, 2 8 1
 + 1, 1 9 8
   7, 4 7 9
```

30.
```
   4, 6 3 3
 + 3, 0 4 7
   7, 6 8 0
```

31.
```
   2, 2 8 2
 + 4, 0 6 0
   6, 3 4 2
```

Singapore Math Level 3A & 3B

32.
$$\begin{array}{r} 3,6\ 3\ 2 \\ +\ 6,2\ 6\ 1 \\ \hline \mathbf{9,8\ 9\ 3} \end{array}$$

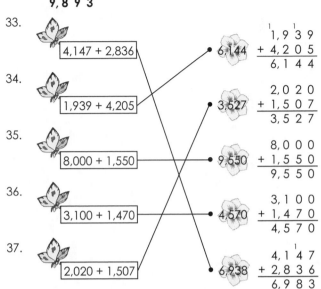

33. 4,147 + 2,836 → 6,983
34. 1,939 + 4,205 → 6,144
35. 8,000 + 1,550 → 9,550
36. 3,100 + 1,470 → 4,570
37. 2,020 + 1,507 → 3,527

$$\begin{array}{r} \overset{1}{1},\overset{1}{9}\ 3\ 9 \\ +\ 4,2\ 0\ 5 \\ \hline 6,1\ 4\ 4 \end{array}$$

$$\begin{array}{r} 2,0\ 2\ 0 \\ +\ 1,5\ 0\ 7 \\ \hline 3,5\ 2\ 7 \end{array}$$

$$\begin{array}{r} 8,0\ 0\ 0 \\ +\ 1,5\ 5\ 0 \\ \hline 9,5\ 5\ 0 \end{array}$$

$$\begin{array}{r} 3,1\ 0\ 0 \\ +\ 1,4\ 7\ 0 \\ \hline 4,5\ 7\ 0 \end{array}$$

$$\begin{array}{r} 4,\overset{1}{1}\ 4\ 7 \\ +\ 2,8\ 3\ 6 \\ \hline 6,9\ 8\ 3 \end{array}$$

38.
3,279	2,580

?

3,279 + 2,580 = 5,859
Both shops sell **5,859** cans of drinks.

$$\begin{array}{r} 3,\overset{1}{2}\ 7\ 9 \\ +\ 2,5\ 8\ 0 \\ \hline 5,8\ 5\ 9 \end{array}$$

39.
$1,574	$3,100

?

$1,574 + $3,100 = $4,674
He spent **$4,674** altogether.

$$\begin{array}{r} 1,5\ 7\ 4 \\ +\ 3,1\ 0\ 0 \\ \hline 4,6\ 7\ 4 \end{array}$$

40. June 4,200 km
July 1,935 km

?

4,200 + 1,935 = 6,135
He travelled **6,135** km in July.

$$\begin{array}{r} \overset{1}{4},2\ 0\ 0 \\ +\ 1,9\ 3\ 5 \\ \hline 6,1\ 3\ 5 \end{array}$$

41. Ben 4,164
William 2,659

?

4,164 + 2,659 = 6,823
William collects **6,823** bottle caps.

$$\begin{array}{r} 4,\overset{1}{1}\ \overset{1}{6}\ 4 \\ +\ 2,6\ 5\ 9 \\ \hline 6,8\ 2\ 3 \end{array}$$

42.
2,347	3,169

?

2,347 + 3,169 = 5,516
He sold **5,516** pens in two months.

$$\begin{array}{r} 2,\overset{1}{3}\ \overset{1}{4}\ 7 \\ +\ 3,1\ 6\ 9 \\ \hline 5,5\ 1\ 6 \end{array}$$

Review 1

1. **one thousand, nine hundred fifteen**
2. **six thousand, three hundred six**
3. **3,012**
4. **8,228**
5.
$$\begin{array}{r} \overset{1}{4},\overset{1}{3}\ 7\ 9 \\ +\ 2,4\ 6\ 8 \\ \hline \mathbf{6,8\ 4\ 7} \end{array}$$

6.
$$\begin{array}{r} \overset{1}{1},\overset{1}{0}\ 0\ 2 \\ +\ 2,8\ 9\ 9 \\ \hline \mathbf{3,9\ 0\ 1} \end{array}$$

7.
$$\begin{array}{r} 5,\overset{1}{3}\ \overset{1}{8}\ 5 \\ +\ 2,4\ 1\ 8 \\ \hline \mathbf{7,8\ 0\ 3} \end{array}$$

8.
$$\begin{array}{r} 4,0\ \overset{1}{1}\ 6 \\ +\ 3,8\ 4\ 9 \\ \hline \mathbf{7,8\ 6\ 5} \end{array}$$

9. **4,798**
10. **1,050**
11. **3,717**
12. **6,203**
13. **4,634, 4,644**
   4,624 − 4,614 = 10
   4,624 + 10 = 4,634
   4,634 + 10 = 4,644
14. **7,918, 7,975**
   7,956 − 7,937 = 19
   7,899 + 19 = 7,918
   7,956 + 19 = 7,975
15. **4,680, 4,860, 6,048, 6,840**
16. (a) **2**
    (b) **6**
    (c) **hundreds**
    (d) **3**
17. 7,096 + 1,845 = **8,941**

$$\begin{array}{r} 7,\overset{1}{0}\ \overset{1}{9}\ 6 \\ +\ 1,8\ 4\ 5 \\ \hline 8,9\ 4\ 1 \end{array}$$

18. **13, 4, 9**
   1, 3, 4, 9
   4 + 9 hundreds 3 + 1 tens 4 + 5 ones
   = 13 hundreds 4 tens 9 ones
   = 1 thousand 3 hundreds 4 tens 9 ones

19. March $4,312
    April $688

?

$4,312 + $688 = $5,000
He saved **$5,000** in April.

$$\begin{array}{r} 4,3\ 1\ 2 \\ +\ \ \ 6\ 8\ 8 \\ \hline 5,0\ 0\ 0 \end{array}$$

20. bracelet $1,375
    necklace $1,999

?

$1,375 + $1,999 = $3,374
Mandy pays **$3,374** for the diamond necklace.

$$\begin{array}{r} \overset{1}{1},\overset{1}{3}\ \overset{1}{7}\ 5 \\ +\ 1,9\ 9\ 9 \\ \hline 3,3\ 7\ 4 \end{array}$$

Unit 3: Subtracting Numbers up to 10,000

1. 67 − 17 = **50**

$$\begin{array}{r} 6\ 7 \\ -\ 1\ 7 \\ \hline 5\ 0 \end{array}$$

2. 53 − 12 = **41**

$$\begin{array}{r} 5\ 3 \\ -\ 1\ 2 \\ \hline 4\ 1 \end{array}$$

3. 548 − 320 = **228**

$$\begin{array}{r} 5\ 4\ 8 \\ -\ 3\ 2\ 0 \\ \hline 2\ 2\ 8 \end{array}$$

4.   486 – 35 = **451**

                      4 8 6
                    –   3 5
                      4 5 1

5.   979 – 546 = **433**

                      9 7 9
                    – 5 4 6
                      4 3 3

6.
```
   3,8 6 9
 –   2 3 5
   3,6 3 4
```

7.
```
   7,7 8 7
 – 4,3 2 5
   3,4 6 2
```

8.
```
   9,7̶7̶ 6
 – 1,0 8 5
   8,6 9 1
```

9.
```
   5,8 8̶1̶
 – 4,0 5 8
   1,8 2 3
```

10.
```
   2,8̶0̶ 0
 –   8 9 0
   2,0 1 0
```

11.
```
   4,1 3̶8̶
 – 2,1 2 8
   2,0 0 8
```

12.
```
   6,8 4 8
 – 2,0 0 5
   4,8 4 3
```

13.
```
   2,4 2 6
 – 1,3 1 0
   1,1 1 6
```

14.
```
   7̶,4̶ 3 1
 – 5,6 1 1
   1,8 2 0
```

15.
```
   8,8 1 8
 – 7,1 0 7
   1,7 1 1
```

16.
```
   9̶,1̶3̶0̶
 – 3,6 8 4
   5,4 4 6
```

17.
```
   8̶,2̶9̶2̶
 – 8,5 0 5
   5,7 8 7
```

18.
```
   5̶,3̶9̶2̶
 – 2,8 8 6
   2,5 0 6
```

19.
```
   4,9 8̶8̶
 – 3,9 6 9
   1,0 1 9
```

20.
```
   9̶,3̶6̶8
 – 1,4 8 7
   7,8 8 1
```

21.
```
   2̶,3̶7̶8̶
 – 1,4 8 7
     8 8 9
```

22.
```
   8̶,0̶0̶0̶
 – 4,6 5 9
   3,3 4 1
```

23.
```
   3̶,5̶7̶8̶
 – 1,8 9 9
   1,6 7 7
```

24.
```
   6̶,0̶0̶5̶
 – 4,7 6 9
   1,2 3 6
```

25.
```
   8̶,0̶1̶0̶
 – 3,8 6 5
   4,1 4 5
```

26.
```
   4,3 6 9
 – 3,1 2 4
   1,2 4 5
```

27.
```
   5,1 3 9
 – 2,0 0 0
   3,1 3 9
```

28.
```
   5̶,3̶5̶3̶
 – 1,5 2 6
   3,8 2 7
```

29.
```
   3̶,3̶5̶0̶
 – 1,5 9 8
   1,7 5 2
```

30.
```
   6,2̶0̶6
 – 2,0 6 2
   4,1 4 4
```

31.

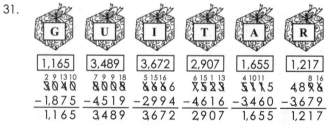

G	U	I	T	A	R
1,165	3,489	3,672	2,907	1,655	1,217

```
   3̶0̶4̶0̶     8̶0̶0̶8̶     6̶6̶6̶6̶     7̶5̶2̶3̶     5̶1̶1̶5̶     4̶8̶9̶6̶
 –1,875   –4,519   –2,994   –4,616   –3,460   –3,679
  1,165    3,489    3,672    2,907    1,655    1,217
```

32.   Hafiz [4,376]
     Alex [?] 2,950

```
   4̶,3̶7 6
 – 2,9 5 0
   1,4 2 6
```

4,376 – 2,950 = 1,426
Alex has **1,426** stickers.

33.   necklace [2,315]
     bracelet [1,670] ?

```
   2̶,3̶1̶5
 – 1,6 7 0
     6 4 5
```

2,315 – 1,670 = 645
She uses **645** fewer beads for the bracelet.

34.   June [5,300]
     July [?] 565

```
   5̶,3̶0̶0̶
 –   5 6 5
   4,7 3 5
```

5,300 – 565 = 4,735
Alicia baked **4,735** muffins in July.

35. TV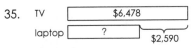

$6,478 − $2,590 = $3,888
The laptop costs **$3,888**.

```
  5 13 17
  6, 4 7 8
− 2, 5 9 0
  3, 8 8 8
```

36.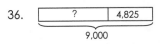

9,000 − 4,825 = 4,175
She sold **4,175** stamps on Monday.

```
  8  9  9 10
  9, 0 0 0
− 4, 8 2 5
  4, 1 7 5
```

Unit 4: Problem Solving (Adding and Subtracting)

1. **(a)**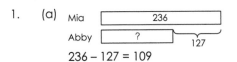

236 − 127 = 109
Abby has **109** stickers.

```
    2 16
  2 3 6
− 1 2 7
  1 0 9
```

(b)
```
236 | 109
```

236 + 109 = 345
They have **345** stickers altogether.

```
    1
  2 3 6
+ 1 0 9
  3 4 5
```

2. Roberto 3,280 mi.
Steve 568 mi.

3,280 + 568 = 3,848
Steve travels 3,848 m.
3,848 + 3,280 = 7,128
They travel **7,128 mi.** altogether.

```
    1
  3, 2 8 0
+    5 6 8
  3, 8 4 8
```
```
  1   1
  3, 8 4 8
+ 3, 2 8 0
  7, 1 2 8
```

3. **(a)** Hailey 2,345
Asia 3,542

3,542 − 2,345 = 1,197
Asia has **1,197** more stamps than Hailey.

```
  4 13 12
  3, 5 4 2
− 2, 3 4 5
  1, 1 9 7
```

(b)
```
3,542 | 2,345
```

3,542 + 2,345 = 5,887
They have **5,887** stamps altogether.

```
  3, 5 4 2
+ 2, 3 4 5
  5, 8 8 7
```

4. Sarah $2,140
Carmen $150
Sonya ? $270

$2,140 + $150 = $2,290
$2,290 − $270 = $2,020
Sonya earns **$2,020**.

```
  2, 1 4 0
+    1 5 0
  2, 2 9 0
```
```
  2, 2 9 0
−    2 7 0
  2, 0 2 0
```

5. **(a)** Rebecca $2,080
Kimiko ? $275

$2,080 − $275 = $1,805
Kimiko pays **$1,805** for her television set.

```
  1 10 7 10
  2, 0 8 0
−    2 7 5
  1, 8 0 5
```

(b)
```
$2,080 | $1,805
```

$2,080 + $1,805 = $3,885
Both television sets cost **$3,885**.

```
  2, 0 8 0
+ 1, 8 0 5
  3, 8 8 5
```

6. girls 3,865
boys 1,459

3,865 + 1,459 = 5,324
5,324 boys went to the concert.

```
  1 1 1
  3, 8 6 5
+ 1, 4 5 9
  5, 3 2 4
```

5,324 + 3,865 = 9,189
9,189 children went to the concert altogether.

```
  1
  5, 3 2 4
+ 3, 8 6 5
  9, 1 8 9
```

7. Saturday 2,015
Sunday 3,585

2,015 + 3,585 = 5,600
5,600 people attended the carnival on Sunday.

```
  2, 0 1 5
+ 3, 5 8 5
  5, 6 0 0
```

5,600 + 2,015 = 7,615
7,615 people attended the carnival on both days.

```
  5, 6 0 0
+ 2, 0 1 5
  7, 6 1 5
```

8. Monday 1,075 kg
Tuesday ? 360 kg

1,075 − 360 = 715
He used 715 kg of cement on Tuesday.

```
  0 10
  1, 0 7 5
−    3 6 0
     7 1 5
```

1,075 + 715 = 1,790
He used **1,790 kg** of cement on both days.

```
       1
  1, 0 7 5
+    7 1 5
  1, 7 9 0
```

9. **(a)** van $5,180
motorcycle $3,960

$5,180 − $3,960 = $1,220
The used motorcycle is **$1,220** less than the used van.

```
  4 11
  5, 1 8 0
− 3, 9 6 0
  1, 2 2 0
```

(b)
```
$5,180 | $3,960
```

$5,180 + $3,960 = $9,140
It will cost **$9,140** to buy the used van and the used motorcycle.

```
  1   1
  5, 1 8 0
+ 3, 9 6 0
  9, 1 4 0
```

10. **(a)** last year $2,387
this year ? $500

$2,387 − $500 = $1,887
Alexandra could spend **$1,887** on books and school supplies this year.

```
  1 13
  2, 3 8 7
−    5 0 0
  1, 8 8 7
```

(b) $4,000
$1,887 ?

$4,000 − $1,887 = $2,113
She would have overspent by **$2,113**.

```
  3  9  9 10
  4, 0 0 0
− 1, 8 8 7
  2, 1 1 3
```

Review 2

1.
```
  8 13 5 18
  9, 3 6 8
− 1, 4 0 9
  7, 9 5 9
```

2.
```
  3 16 15
  4, 7 5 5
− 1, 8 9 0
  2, 8 6 5
```

Singapore Math Level 3A & 3B

3.
8,111
− 2,401
5,710

4.
6,000
− 2,819
3,181

5. **3**
3,789
+ 5,747
9,536

6. **5**
1,173
+ 4,371
5,544

7. **4,217**
6,865
− 2,648
4,217

8. **1,115**
2,865
− 1,750
1,115

9. **4,889**
5,900
− 1,011
4,889

10. **3,900**
4,000
− 100
3,900

11. **6,930**
6,940
− 10
6,930

12. **7,550**
8,000
− 450
7,550

13. **5,550**
5,050
+ 500
5,550

14. **R**
6,389
− 4,693
1,696

E
8,200
− 3,865
4,335

U
3,487
− 1,509
1,978

N
7,777
− 5,998
1,779

T
2,415
+ 1,596
4,011

A
5,189
+ 2,690
7,879

B
4,444
+ 2,055
6,499

P
1,090
+ 2,895
3,985

P	E	A	N	U	T
3,985	4,335	7,879	1,779	1,978	4,011

B	U	T	T	E	R
6,499	1,978	4,011	4,011	4,335	1,696

15. (a)
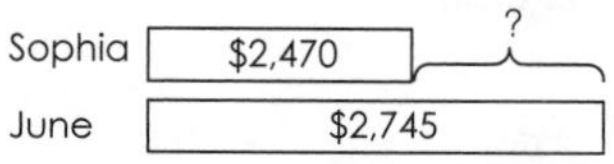

Sophia
$2,470
?
June
$2,745

2,745
− 2,470
275

$2,745 – $2,470 = $275
June earns **$275** more than Sophia.

(b)
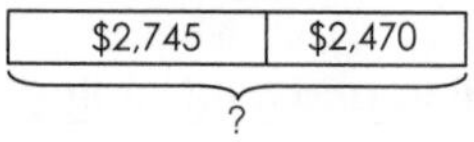

$2,745
$2,470
?

2,745
+ 2,470
5,215

$2,745 + $2,470 = $5,215
They earn **$5,215** altogether.

16.
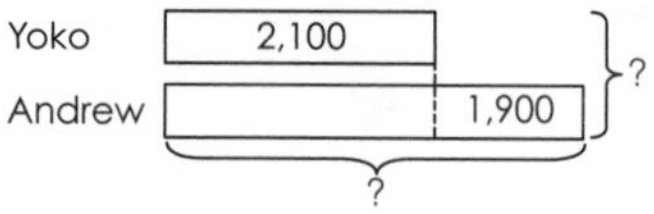

Yoko
2,100
Andrew
1,900
?
?

2,100
+ 1,900
4,000

2,100 + 1,900 = 4,000
Andrew has 4,000 stamps.

4,000
+ 2,100
6,100

4,000 + 2,100 = 6,100
They have **6,100** stamps altogether.

17.
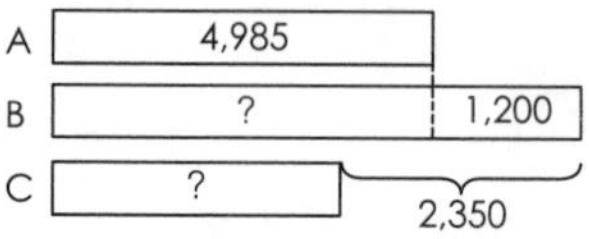

A
4,985
B
?
1,200
C
?
2,350

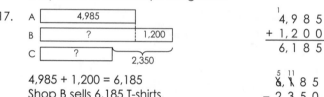

4,985
+ 1,200
6,185

6,185
− 2,350
3,835

4,985 + 1,200 = 6,185
Shop B sells 6,185 T-shirts.
6,185 – 2,350 = 3,835
Shop C sells **3,835** T-shirts.

18.
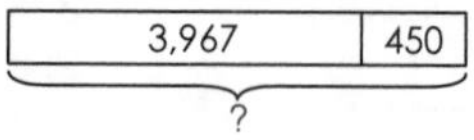

3,967
450
?

3,967
+ 450
4,417

3,967 + 450 = 4,417
Jake has 4,417 stickers.

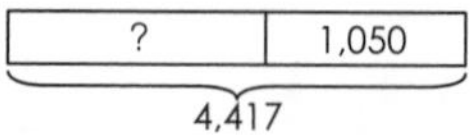

?
1,050
4,417

4,417
− 1,050
3,367

4,417 – 1,050 = 3,367
Jake has **3,367** stickers left.

19.
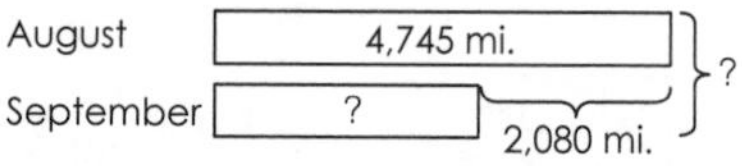

August
4,745 mi.
September
?
2,080 mi.
?

4,745
− 2,080
2,665

4,745 – 2,080 = 2,665
He drove 2,665 km in September.

4,745
+ 2,665
7,410

4,745 + 2,665 = 7,410
Raj's total driving distance in these 2 months was **7,410 mi.**

20. (a)
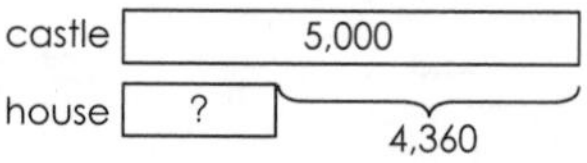

castle
5,000
house
?
4,360

5,000
− 4,360
640

5,000 – 4,360 = 640
He used **640** wooden blocks to build the house.

(b)
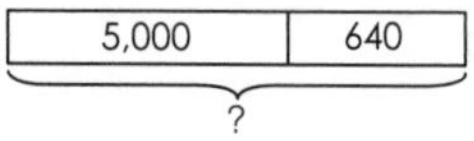

5,000
640
?

5,000
+ 640
5,640

5,000 + 640 = 5,640
He used **5,640** wooden blocks altogether.

Unit 5: Multiplying Numbers by 6, 7, 8, and 9

1. **12**
    6 + 6 = 12
2. **30**
    6 + 6 + 6 + 6 + 6 = 30
3. **10**
    8 + 8 + 8 + 8 + 8 + 8 + 8 + 8 + 8 + 8 = 80
4. **8**
    7 + 7 + 7 + 7 + 7 + 7 + 7 + 7 = 56
5. **81**
    9 + 9 + 9 + 9 + 9 + 9 + 9 + 9 + 9 = 81
6. **5**
    8 + 8 + 8 + 8 + 8 = 40
7. **32**
    8 + 8 + 8 + 8 = 32
8. **4**
    6 + 6 + 6 + 6 = 24
9. **21**
    7 + 7 + 7 = 21
10. **49**
    7 + 7 + 7 + 7 + 7 + 7 + 7 = 49
11. **45**
    9 + 9 + 9 + 9 + 9 = 45
12. **8**
    9 + 9 + 9 + 9 + 9 + 9 + 9 + 9 = 72
13. **8**
    8 + 8 + 8 + 8 + 8 + 8 + 8 + 8 = 64
14. **6**
    8 + 8 + 8 + 8 + 8 + 8 = 48
15. **0**
    Any number multiplied by 0 equals to 0.

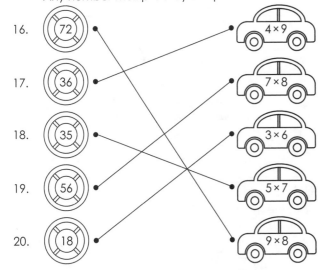

16. 72
17. 36
18. 35
19. 56
20. 18

    4 × 9
    7 × 8
    3 × 6
    5 × 7
    9 × 8

21. (a) **7, 7**
        14
        49
    (b) **6, 6, 6**
        18
        48
    (c) **8, 8, 8**
        24
        64
22. (a) **80, 8**
        72
    (b) **60, 6**
        54

23. **7, 4, 28**
24. **4, 8, 32**
25. **6, 6, 36**
26. **7, 7, 49**
27. **7, 8, 56**
28. **8 × 9 = 72**
    9 × 8 = 72
    72 ÷ 8 = 9
    72 ÷ 9 = 8
29. **6 × 7 = 42**
    7 × 6 = 42
    42 ÷ 6 = 7
    42 ÷ 7 = 6
30. **9 × 6 = 54**
    6 × 9 = 54
    54 ÷ 9 = 6
    54 ÷ 6 = 9
31. **6 × 5 = 30**
    5 × 6 = 30
    30 ÷ 6 = 5
    30 ÷ 5 = 6
32. **9 × 4 = 36**
    4 × 9 = 36
    36 ÷ 9 = 4
    36 ÷ 4 = 9
33. ?
    | 8 | 8 | 8 | 8 | 8 | 8 |
    6 × 8 = 48
    She bought **48** oranges altogether.
34. ?
    | $6 | $6 | $6 | $6 | $6 |
    5 × $6 = $30
    Andy pays **$30** for all the books.
35. ?
    | 5 | 5 | 5 | 5 | 5 | 5 | 5 |
    7 × 5 = 35
    There are **35** people in the group.
36. ?
    | 8 | 8 | 8 | 8 | 8 | 8 | 8 | 8 | 8 |
    9 × 8 = 72
    Elizabeth bakes **72** muffins altogether.
37. 42
    | ? | ? | ? | ? | ? | ? | ? |
    42 ÷ 7 = 6
    Each of them has **6** stickers.
38. 64
    | ? | ? | ? | ? | ? | ? | ? | ? |
    64 ÷ 8 = 8
    There were **8** apples in each bag.

Unit 6: Multiplying Numbers

1.   1 2
       ×   3
       ─────
         3 6

2.
```
    1 1 2
  ×     4
  ───────
    4 4 8
```

3.
```
      3 3
  ×     2
  ───────
      6 6
```

4.
```
    2 1 0
  ×     2
  ───────
    4 2 0
```

5.
```
    3 0 2
  ×     3
  ───────
    9 0 6
```

6.
```
    4 4 2
  ×     2
  ───────
    8 8 4
```

7.
```
    2 1 2
  ×     4
  ───────
    8 4 8
```

8.
```
      3 1
  ×     3
  ───────
      9 3
```

9.
```
    1 0 0
  ×     3
  ───────
    3 0 0
```

10.
```
    1 2 1
  ×     4
  ───────
    4 8 4
```

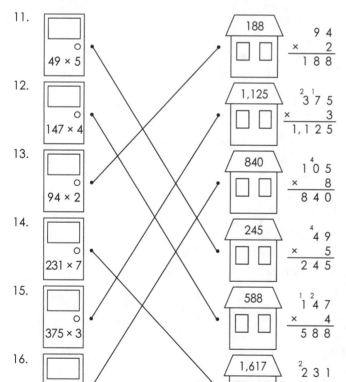

11. 49 × 5
12. 147 × 4
13. 94 × 2
14. 231 × 7
15. 375 × 3
16. 105 × 8

188
```
      9 4
  ×     2
  ───────
    1 8 8
```

1,125
```
    ²3¹7 5
  ×     3
  ───────
  1,1 2 5
```

840
```
    1 0⁴5
  ×     8
  ───────
    8 4 0
```

245
```
    ⁴4 9
  ×   5
  ───────
    2 4 5
```

588
```
    ¹4 7²
  ×     4
  ───────
    5 8 8
```

1,617
```
    ²2 3 1
  ×       7
  ───────
  1,6 1 7
```

17.

	(a) 8	9	(f) 6		(b) 7	1	1
(g) 6		(c) 3	1	0			
1			7		(h) 3		
2			(d) 8	5	6		
(i) 8		(j) 6		(e) 8	2	6	
8		4					
2		0					

(a)
```
    1¹ 2
  ×     8
  ───────
    8 9 6
```

(f)
```
      9 1
  ×     7
  ───────
    6 3 7
```

(b)
```
    ⁸7 9
  ×     9
  ───────
    7 1 1
```

(g)
```
    1 0²
  ×     6
  ───────
    6 1 2
```

(c)
```
    ¹6 2
  ×     5
  ───────
    3 1 0
```

(h)
```
    ⁴4 6
  ×     8
  ───────
    3 6 8
```

(d)
```
    2¹ 4
  ×     4
  ───────
    8 5 6
```

(i)
```
    ⁷9 8
  ×     9
  ───────
    8 8 2
```

(e)
```
    ¹1 ⁵8
  ×     7
  ───────
    8 2 6
```

(j)
```
      8 0
  ×     8
  ───────
    6 4 0
```

18.
```
  ²5³3 7      4³1 6      ²1 3²3      6 0 0      ²2 0 4
×     6    ×     5    ×     7    ×     2    ×     5
───────    ───────    ───────    ───────    ───────
  3,2 2 2    2,0 8 0      9 3 1    1,2 0 0    1,0 2 0

  ¹7⁴3      ⁷3 9 1      ⁶1 6⁸9      8²2 4
×     4    ×     8    ×     9    ×     3
───────    ───────    ───────    ───────
  2,9 7 2    3,1 2 8    1,5 2 1    2,4 7 2
```

B	O	B	O	T	H	E
1,200	2,080	1,200	2,080	3,128	3,222	1,020

C	L	O	W	N
2,472	2,972	2,080	931	1,521

19.
```
         ?
  ┌──┬──┬──┬──┬──┬──┐
  │15│15│15│15│15│15│
  └──┴──┴──┴──┴──┴──┘
```
```
    ³1 5
  ×   6
  ─────
    9 0
```
6 × 15 = 90
There were **90** colored pencils altogether.

20.
```
         ?
  ┌────┬────┬────┐
  │230 │230 │230 │
  └────┴────┴────┘
```
```
    2 3 0
  ×     3
  ───────
    6 9 0
```
230 × 3 = 690
The total number of people who went to the concert was **690**.

21.
```
         ?
  ┌─────┬─────┬─────┐
  │$637 │$637 │$637 │
  └─────┴─────┴─────┘
```
```
    ¹6²3 7
  ×       3
  ───────
    1,9 1 1
```
$637 × 3 = $1,911
He spent **$1,911** at the electronics store.

22.
```
              ?
  ┌──────┬──────┬──────┬──────┬──────┐
  │750 mL│750 mL│750 mL│750 mL│750 mL│
  └──────┴──────┴──────┴──────┴──────┘
```
```
    ²7 5 0
  ×       5
  ───────
    3,7 5 0
```
750 × 5 = 3,750

236

Singapore Math Level 3A & 3B

The total volume of syrup that Brittany bought was **3,750 mL**.

23.

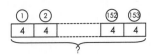

$$\begin{array}{r} {}^{2}1\,{}^{1}5\,3 \\ \times \qquad 4 \\ \hline 6\,1\,2 \end{array}$$

$153 \times 4 = 612$
There were **612** wheels altogether.

Review 3

1. **$5 \times 8 = 40$**
    $8 \times 5 = 40$
    $40 \div 5 = 8$
    $40 \div 8 = 5$

2. **$7 \times 4 = 28$**
    $4 \times 7 = 28$
    $28 \div 7 = 4$
    $28 \div 4 = 7$

3. $$\begin{array}{r} {}^{3}1\,{}^{5}4\,7 \\ \times \qquad 8 \\ \hline 1,1\,7\,6 \end{array}$$

4. $$\begin{array}{r} 3\,1\,2 \\ \times \qquad 3 \\ \hline 9\,3\,6 \end{array}$$

5. $$\begin{array}{r} {}^{1}6\,3\,2 \\ \times \qquad 4 \\ \hline 2,5\,2\,8 \end{array}$$

6. $$\begin{array}{r} 5\,0\,0 \\ \times \qquad 3 \\ \hline 1,5\,0\,0 \end{array}$$

7. **5, 9, 45**

8.
9.
10.
11.
12.

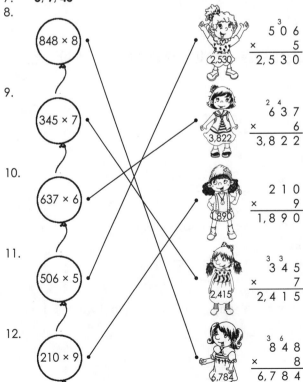

13. **54**
    $6 + 6 + 6 + 6 + 6 + 6 + 6 + 6 + 6 = 54$

14. **7**
    $8 + 8 + 8 + 8 + 8 + 8 + 8 = 56$

15. **7**
    $7 + 7 + 7 + 7 = 28$

16. **7**
    $9 + 9 + 9 + 9 + 9 + 9 + 9 = 63$

17.
```
          ?
| 139 | 139 | 139 | 139 | 139 | 139 | 139 | 139 |
```
$$\begin{array}{r} {}^{3}1\,{}^{7}3\,9 \\ \times \qquad 8 \\ \hline 1,1\,1\,2 \end{array}$$

$139 \times 8 = 1,112$
She needs **1,112** beads to make 8 such bags.

18.
```
         ?
| 235 | 235 | 235 | 235 | 235 | 235 | 235 |
```
$$\begin{array}{r} {}^{2}2\,{}^{3}3\,5 \\ \times \qquad 7 \\ \hline 1,6\,4\,5 \end{array}$$

$235 \times 7 = 1,645$
He has **1,645** stamps altogether.

19.
```
               54
| ? | ? | ? | ? | ? | ? | ? | ? | ? |
```
$54 \div 9 = 6$
There were **6** ribbons in each packet.

20.

```
 ①   ②          44   45
| 5 | 5 | --- | 5 | 5 |
         ?
```
$$\begin{array}{r} {}^{2}4\,5 \\ \times \qquad 5 \\ \hline 2\,2\,5 \end{array}$$

$45 \times 5 = 225$
45 cars can transport **225** people.

Unit 7: Dividing Numbers

1. **9, 4**
    $$\begin{array}{r} 9 \\ 7\overline{)67} \\ \underline{63} \\ 4 \end{array}$$

2. **3, 2**
    $$\begin{array}{r} 3 \\ 5\overline{)17} \\ \underline{15} \\ 2 \end{array}$$

3. **8, 1**
    $$\begin{array}{r} 8 \\ 3\overline{)25} \\ \underline{24} \\ 1 \end{array}$$

4. **9, 7**
    $$\begin{array}{r} 9 \\ 9\overline{)88} \\ \underline{81} \\ 7 \end{array}$$

5. **7, 1**
    $$\begin{array}{r} 7 \\ 4\overline{)29} \\ \underline{28} \\ 1 \end{array}$$

6. **8, 4**
    $$\begin{array}{r} 8 \\ 6\overline{)52} \\ \underline{48} \\ 4 \end{array}$$

7. **234, 1**
    $$\begin{array}{r} 234 \\ 2\overline{)469} \\ \underline{4} \\ 6 \\ \underline{6} \\ 9 \\ \underline{8} \\ 1 \end{array}$$

8. **18**

```
      18
   5)90
      5
      40
      40
       0
```

9. **28**

```
      28
   3)84
      6
      24
      24
       0
```

10. **99**

```
      99
   8)792
      72
      72
      72
       0
```

11. **91**

```
      91
   7)637
      63
       7
       7
       0
```

12. **23**

```
      23
   6)138
      12
      18
      18
       0
```

13. **234**

```
     234
   3)702
      6
      10
       9
      12
      12
       0
```

14. **108**

```
     108
   9)972
      9
      7
      0
      72
      72
       0
```

15. **203**

```
     203
   4)812
      8
      1
      0
      12
      12
       0
```

16.

```
    8         6         8         7         9
  2)17      8)55      7)60      6)43      4)38
    16        48        56        42        36
     1         7         4         1         2
```

C	A	M	E	R	A
8 R 4	9 R 2	8 R 1	6 R 7	7 R 1	9 R 2

17.

```
    11        13        10        24        12        32
  2)22      3)39      2)20      2)48      4)48      2)64
    2         3         2         4         4         6
    2         9         0         8         8         4
    2         9         0         8         8         4
    0         0         0         0         0         0
```

M	U	S	H	R	O	O	M
13	32	24	12	11	10	10	13

18. (a) **1, 3, 5, 7, 9**
    (b) **2, 4, 6, 8**
19. **16, 48, 74, 56, 82, 20**
20. **11, 49, 65, 7, 83, 91, 37**
21. **9,730**
22. **1,245**

23.

426
| ? | ? | ? | ? | ? | ? |

```
      71
   6)426
      42
       6
       6
       0
```

426 ÷ 6 = 71
There were **71** paperclips in each box.

24.

| 4 | 4 | ⋯ | 4 | 4 |

958

```
     239
   4)958
      8
      15
      12
      38
      36
       2
```

958 ÷ 4 = 239 R 2
He manufactured **239** cars in June.

25.

| 5 | 5 | ⋯ | 5 | 5 |

167

```
      33
   5)167
      15
      17
      15
       2
```

167 ÷ 5 = 33 R 2

(a) She has **33** students in her class.
(b) She has **2** muffins left.

Unit 8: Problem Solving (Multiplying and Dividing)

1.

?
| $135 | $135 |

$135 × 2 = $270
Linh saved **$270** in March.

```
      1
     135
   ×   2
     270
```

2.

Brooke | 484 |

Annie | 484 | 484 | 484 | 484 |
?

484 × 4 = 1,936
Annie bakes **1,936** dog biscuits.

```
    3 1
     484
   ×   4
   1,936
```

3.

Wednesday | 187 |

Weekend | 187 | 187 | 187 |
?

187 × 3 = 561
561 people watched the movie that weekend.

```
    2 2
     187
   ×   3
     561
```

4.

A | 565 |

B | 565 | 565 |
?

565 × 2 = 1,130
Bakery B sold **1,130** loaves of bread.

```
    1 1
     565
   ×   2
   1,130
```

5.
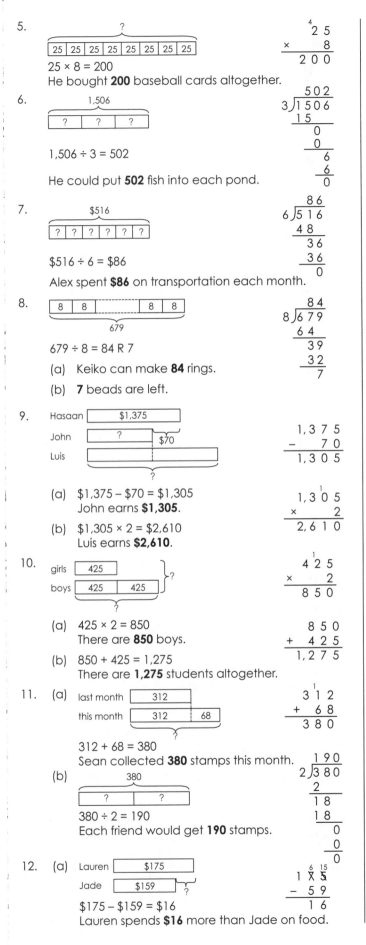

25 × 8 = 200
He bought **200** baseball cards altogether.

$$\begin{array}{r} {}^{4}2\,5 \\ \times\quad 8 \\ \hline 2\,0\,0 \end{array}$$

6.
1,506 ÷ 3 = 502

He could put **502** fish into each pond.

$$3\overline{)1506} = 502$$

7.
$516 ÷ 6 = $86

Alex spent **$86** on transportation each month.

$$6\overline{)516} = 86$$

8.
679 ÷ 8 = 84 R 7

(a) Keiko can make **84** rings.

(b) **7** beads are left.

$$8\overline{)679} = 84\ R\ 7$$

9.
Hasaan $1,375
John ? $70
Luis

(a) $1,375 − $70 = $1,305
John earns **$1,305**.

(b) $1,305 × 2 = $2,610
Luis earns **$2,610**.

$$\begin{array}{r} 1,3\,7\,5 \\ -\quad 7\,0 \\ \hline 1,3\,0\,5 \end{array} \qquad \begin{array}{r} 1,3\,0\,5 \\ \times\quad 2 \\ \hline 2,6\,1\,0 \end{array}$$

10.
girls 425
boys 425 425

(a) 425 × 2 = 850
There are **850** boys.

(b) 850 + 425 = 1,275
There are **1,275** students altogether.

$$\begin{array}{r} {}^{1}4\,2\,5 \\ \times\quad 2 \\ \hline 8\,5\,0 \end{array} \qquad \begin{array}{r} 8\,5\,0 \\ +\quad 4\,2\,5 \\ \hline 1,2\,7\,5 \end{array}$$

11. (a)
last month 312
this month 312 68

312 + 68 = 380
Sean collected **380** stamps this month.

$$\begin{array}{r} {}^{1}3\,1\,2 \\ +\quad 6\,8 \\ \hline 3\,8\,0 \end{array}$$

(b)
380
? ?

380 ÷ 2 = 190
Each friend would get **190** stamps.

$$2\overline{)380} = 190$$

12. (a)
Lauren $175
Jade $159 ?

$175 − $159 = $16
Lauren spends **$16** more than Jade on food.

$$\begin{array}{r} {}^{6}1\,{}^{15}\!\cancel{7}\,\cancel{5} \\ -\quad 5\,9 \\ \hline 1\,6 \end{array}$$

(b)
$16 × 6 = $96
Lauren spends **$96** more on food than Jade in 6 months.

$$\begin{array}{r} {}^{3}1\,6 \\ \times\quad 6 \\ \hline 9\,6 \end{array}$$

13. (a)
98 × 2 = 196
Mr. McKay travels **196 km** to and from the city.

$$\begin{array}{r} {}^{1}9\,8 \\ \times\quad 2 \\ \hline 1\,9\,6 \end{array}$$

(b)
196 × 7 = 1,372
He will travel **1,372 km** in all.

$$\begin{array}{r} {}^{6}{}^{4}1\,9\,6 \\ \times\quad 7 \\ \hline 1,3\,7\,2 \end{array}$$

14. (a)
$160 × 6 = $960
Emelda saved **$960** in half a year.

$$\begin{array}{r} {}^{3}1\,6\,0 \\ \times\quad 6 \\ \hline 9\,6\,0 \end{array}$$

(b)
$960
? ? ? ? ? ? ? ?

$960 ÷ 8 = $120
The cost of each present was **$120**.

$$8\overline{)960} = 120$$

15. (a)
6 × 8 = 48
She uses **48 yd.** of fabric in a week.

(b)
100 yds.
48 ?

100 − 48 = 52
She has **52 yd.** of fabric left.

$$\begin{array}{r} {}^{0}{}^{9}{}^{10}\!\cancel{1}\,\cancel{0}\,\cancel{0} \\ -\quad 4\,8 \\ \hline 5\,2 \end{array}$$

16.
25 × 9 = 225
There were 225 crayons altogether.

$$\begin{array}{r} {}^{4}2\,5 \\ \times\quad 9 \\ \hline 2\,2\,5 \end{array}$$

225 ÷ 5 = 45
She had **45** students.

$$5\overline{)225} = 45$$

17.
24 × 3 = 72
There were 72 apples altogether.

$$\begin{array}{r} {}^{1}2\,4 \\ \times\quad 3 \\ \hline 7\,2 \end{array}$$

72 + 245 = 317
She bought **317** pieces of fruit altogether.

$$\begin{array}{r} {}^{1}2\,4\,5 \\ +\quad 7\,2 \\ \hline 3\,1\,7 \end{array}$$

18.
radio $95 $95
TV $190

$95 × 2 = $190
$190 × 2 = $380
He needs **$380**.

$$\begin{array}{r} {}^{1}9\,5 \\ \times\quad 2 \\ \hline 1\,9\,0 \end{array} \qquad \begin{array}{r} {}^{1}1\,9\,0 \\ \times\quad 2 \\ \hline 3\,8\,0 \end{array}$$

19.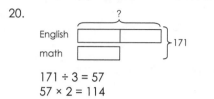

$$\begin{array}{r} 7\overset{2}{5} \\ \times \quad 4 \\ \hline 3\,0\,0 \end{array}$$

$75 \times 4 = \$300$

Charley paid **$300** for the furniture.

20.

English | | | ⎫
math | | | ⎬ 171

$$\begin{array}{r} 5\,7 \\ 3\overline{)1\,7\,1} \\ \underline{1\,5} \\ 2\,1 \\ \underline{2\,1} \\ 0 \end{array} \qquad \begin{array}{r} \overset{1}{5}\,7 \\ \times \quad 2 \\ \hline 1\,1\,4 \end{array}$$

$171 \div 3 = 57$
$57 \times 2 = 114$

She scored **114** points in English.

Unit 9: Mental Calculations

1. **89**
   $65 + 20 = 85$
   $85 + 4 = 89$
2. **52**
   $40 + 13 = 53$
   $53 - 1 = 52$
3. **134**
   $56 + 80 = 136$
   $136 - 2 = 134$
4. **128**
   $84 + 40 = 124$
   $124 + 4 = 128$
5. **99**
   $74 + 20 = 94$
   $94 + 5 = 99$
6. **118**
   $31 + 80 = 111$
   $111 + 7 = 118$
7. **90**
   $42 + 50 = 92$
   $92 - 2 = 0$
8. **158**
   $61 + 100 = 161$
   $161 - 3 = 158$
9. **86**
   $57 + 30 = 87$
   $87 - 1 = 86$
10. **77**
    $20 + 58 = 78$
    $78 - 1 = 77$
11. **31**
    $49 - 10 = 39$
    $39 - 8 = 31$
12. **21**
    $74 - 50 = 24$
    $24 - 3 = 21$
13. **45**
    $64 - 20 = 44$
    $44 + 1 = 45$
14. **55**
    $83 - 30 = 53$
    $53 + 2 = 55$
15. **28**
    $37 - 10 = 27$
    $27 + 1 = 28$

16. **39**
    $86 - 50 = 36$
    $36 + 3 = 39$
17. **27**
    $62 - 40 = 22$
    $22 + 5 = 27$
18. **31**
    $77 - 50 = 27$
    $27 + 4 = 31$
19. **49**
    $96 - 50 = 46$
    $46 + 3 = 49$
20. **28**
    $55 - 30 = 25$
    $25 + 3 = 28$
21. **40**
22. **81**
23. **21**
24. **18**
25. **28**
26. **18**
27. **480**
    8×6 tens = 48 tens = 480
28. **420**
    6×7 tens = 42 tens = 420
29. **1,200**
    3×4 hundreds =
    12 hundreds = 1,200
30. **2,500**
    5×5 hundreds =
    25 hundreds = 2,500
31. **8**
    $3 \times 8 = 24$
32. **9**
    $6 \times 9 = 54$
33. **10**
    $5 \times 10 = 50$
34. **9**
    $8 \times 9 = 72$
35. **10**
    $10 \times 9 = 90$
36. **20**
    8 tens $\div 4$ = 2 tens = 20
37. **50**
    35 tens $\div 7$ = 5 tens = 50
38. **70**
    21 tens $\div 3$ = 7 tens = 70
39. **60**
    36 tens $\div 6$ = 6 tens = 60
40. **40**
    16 tens $\div 4$ = 4 tens = 40

Review 4

1. **76, 5**

$$\begin{array}{r} 7\,6 \\ 7\overline{)5\,3\,7} \\ \underline{4\,9} \\ 4\,7 \\ \underline{4\,2} \\ 5 \end{array}$$

Singapore Math Level 3A & 3B

2. **102**

```
    1 0 2
6 )6 1 2
    6
    1
    0
    1 2
    1 2
        0
```

3. **100**, **8**

```
    1 0 0
9 )9 0 8
    9
    0
    0
    8
    0
    8
```

4. **126**

```
    1 2 6
4 )5 0 4
    4
    1 0
      8
    2 4
    2 4
      0
```

5. **2,358**
6. **9,843**

7.
```
    5 1        3 1 8       1 1 9       2 0 6       1 3 5        7 9
7 )3 5 7    3 )9 5 4    6 )7 1 4    4 )8 2 4    5 )6 7 5    9 )7 1 1
    3 5         9           6           8           5           6 3
      7         5           1 1         2           1 7         8 1
      7         3           6           0           1 5         8 1
      0         2 4         5 4         2 4         2 5           0
                2 4         5 4         2 4         2 5
                  0           0           0           0
```

L	I	B	R	A	R	Y
79	51	318	206	135	206	119

8. **139**

```
    1 3 9
2 )2 7 8
    2
    7
    6
    1 8
    1 8
      0
```

9. **106**

37 + 70 = 107

107 − 1 = 106

10. **51**, **53**, **55**, **57**, **59**

11. **15**

34 − 20 = 14

14 + 1 = 15

12. **50**

```
      5 0
8 )4 0 0
    4 0
      0
      0
      0
```

13. **32**, **34**, **36**, **38**, **40**

14. **40**

15. **4**

24 ÷ 6 = 4

16. (a)

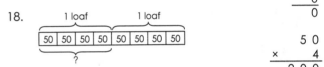

4 × 5 = 20

There are **20** packets of noodles altogether.

(b)

2	2	...	2	2

20

20 ÷ 2 = 10

She gives the noodles to **10** friends.

17.

230	230	230	230	230	230

```
      1
    2 3 0
  ×     6
  1,3 8 0
```

230 × 6 = 1,380

There are **1,380** stamps altogether.

1,380

?	?	?

```
      4 6 0
3 )1,3 8 0
    1 2
      1 8
      1 8
        0
        0
        0
```

1,380 ÷ 3 = 460

Each nephew receives **460** stamps.

18.

1 loaf   1 loaf

50	50	50	50	50	50	50	50

?

```
      5 0
  ×     4
  2 0 0
```

50 × 4 = 200

She needs **200 g** of sugar for each loaf of banana bread.

19.

$27

A | ? | ? | ? |

B | ? | ? | ? | ? | ? |

$40

$27 ÷ 3 = $9

$40 ÷ 5 = $8

Shop B sells the toy at a cheaper price.

20. (a)

464 yd.

?	?

```
      2 3 2
2 )4 6 4
    4
    6
    6
    4
    4
    0
```

464 ÷ 2 = 232

Nick's house is **232 yd.** from the city.

(b)

464	464	464	464	464

?

```
    3 2
    4 6 4
  ×     5
  2,3 2 0
```

464 × 5 = 2,320

Nick would travel **2,320 yd.** in 5 days.

Mid-Review

1. **7,300**
2. **4,040**
3. **five thousand, fifteen**
4. **six thousand, four hundred eleven**
5.
```
    1     1
    3, 6  1 8
  + 2, 9  3 4
    6, 5  5 2
```

6.
$$\overset{3}{\cancel{4}}\,\overset{13}{\cancel{3}}\,\overset{6}{\cancel{7}}\,\overset{12}{\cancel{2}}$$
$$-\;2,4\,6\,5$$
$$\overline{\;\;\;1,9\,0\,7}$$

7.
$$\overset{3}{1}\,\overset{6}{4}\,9$$
$$\times\qquad 7$$
$$\overline{1,0\,4\,3}$$

8. **7**
$$\begin{array}{r}1\,0\,7\\8\overline{)8\,6\,3}\\8\\\hline 6\\0\\\hline 6\,3\\5\,6\\\hline 7\end{array}$$

9. **41**
20 + 25 = 45
45 − 4 = 41

10.
$$\overset{1}{3},\overset{1}{8}\,9\,1$$
$$+\;4,6\,2\,3$$
$$\overline{8,5\,1\,4}$$

11.
$$\overset{8}{\cancel{9}}\,\overset{9}{\cancel{0}}\,\overset{9}{\cancel{0}}\,\overset{10}{\cancel{0}}$$
$$-\;4,5\,1\,5$$
$$\overline{4,4\,8\,5}$$

12.
$$\begin{array}{r}1\,1\,4\\7\overline{)8\,0\,0}\\7\\\hline 1\,0\\7\\\hline 3\,0\\2\,8\\\hline \mathbf{2}\end{array}$$

13.
$$\overset{7}{\cancel{8}}\,\overset{11}{\cancel{2}}\,\overset{12}{\cancel{3}}\,\overset{10}{\cancel{0}}$$
$$-\;1,9\,6\,5$$
$$\overline{6,2\,6\,5}$$

14.
$$\overset{1}{4}\,\overset{3}{1}\,4$$
$$\times\qquad 8$$
$$\overline{3,3\,1\,2}$$

15.
$$\begin{array}{r}7\,8\\4\overline{)3\,1\,2}\\2\,8\\\hline 3\,2\\3\,2\\\hline 0\end{array}$$

16. **2,436, 4,263, 6,302, 8,143**
17. **greater**
18. **6 × 7 = 42**
     7 × 6 = 42
     42 ÷ 6 = 7
     42 ÷ 7 = 6
19. **2,117, 2,217**
     2,417 − 2,317 = 100
     2,017 + 100 = 2,117
     2,117 + 100 = 2,217
20. **8, 3, 24**

21.
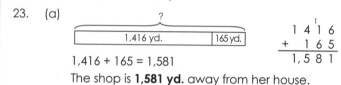
55 × 8 = 440
There are 440 seashells altogether.

440 ÷ 2 = 220
There are **220** seashells in each bag.

$$\begin{array}{r}\overset{4}{5}\,5\\\times\quad 8\\\hline 4\,4\,0\end{array}\qquad\begin{array}{r}2\,2\,0\\2\overline{)4\,4\,0}\\4\\\hline 4\\4\\\hline 0\\0\\\hline 0\end{array}$$

22. Carson [316]
     James [316 | 316 | 316]
     Dan [?]⌣400
     316 × 3 = 948
     948 − 400 = 548
     Dan has **548** bottle caps.
$$\begin{array}{r}3\,\overset{1}{1}\,6\\\times\qquad 3\\\hline 9\,4\,8\end{array}$$
$$\begin{array}{r}9\,4\,8\\-\;4\,0\,0\\\hline 5\,4\,8\end{array}$$

23. (a)
     [1,416 yd. | 165 yd.]
     1,416 + 165 = 1,581
     The shop is **1,581 yd.** away from her house.
$$\begin{array}{r}1\,\overset{1}{4}\,1\,6\\+\quad 1\,6\,5\\\hline 1,5\,8\,1\end{array}$$

     (b)
     [1,581 yd. | 1,581 yd.]
     1,581 × 2 = 3,162
     She walks **3,162 yd.**
$$\begin{array}{r}\overset{1}{1}\,5\,\overset{1}{8}\,1\\\times\qquad 2\\\hline 3,1\,6\,2\end{array}$$

24. 138 km
     [? | ?]
     138 ÷ 2 = 69
     She will travel **69 km**.
$$\begin{array}{r}6\,9\\2\overline{)1\,3\,8}\\1\,2\\\hline 1\,8\\1\,8\\\hline 0\end{array}$$

25.
     [$1,450 | $1,450]
     $1,450 × 2 = $2,900
     Monica paid **$2,900** for the entertainment center.
$$\begin{array}{r}\overset{1}{1}\,4\,5\,0\\\times\qquad 2\\\hline 2,9\,0\,0\end{array}$$

     $5,000
     [$2,900 | $1,450 | ?]
     $2,900 + $1,450 = $4,350
     $5,000 − $4,350 = $650
     She would receive **$650** in change.
$$\begin{array}{r}\overset{1}{2},9\,0\,0\\+\;1,4\,5\,0\\\hline 4,3\,5\,0\end{array}$$
$$\begin{array}{r}\overset{4}{\cancel{5}},\overset{9}{\cancel{0}}\,\overset{10}{\cancel{0}}\,0\\-\;4,3\,5\,0\\\hline 6\,5\,0\end{array}$$

Challenge Questions

1. $6 + $12 + $18 + $24 + $30 + $36 + $42 = $168
    He will save **$168** by Sunday.

2. Starting from the third term, the result of each term is obtained by adding its 2 preceding numbers.
    47 + 29 = **76**
    76 + 47 = **123**
    123 + 76 = **199**

Singapore Math Level 3A & 3B

3.

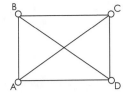

A shook hands with B, C, and D. (3 handshakes)

B shook hands with C and D. (2 handshakes)

C shook hands with D. (1 handshake)

3 + 2 + 1 = 6 handshakes

4 people were at the party.

4. The possible combinations of the 2-digit numbers are 12, 13, 21, 23, 31, and 32.
The 2-digit numbers that can be divided by 4 are **12** and **32**.

5. Let the digits be A, B, C, and D.

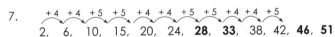

$$A \qquad \underline{B} \qquad \underline{C} \qquad D$$
$$\text{smallest} \quad \text{biggest}$$

(C + D) – (A + B) = 8

A + B + C + D = 26

Use the guess-and-check method.

C + D = 9 + 8 = 17

A + B = 5 + 4 = 9

17 – 9 = 8

5 + 4 + 9 + 8 = 26

Number X is **5,498**.

6. When divided by 5, the number could be 22, 27, (32), or 37.
When divided by 6, the number could be 26, (32), or 38.

32 ÷ 5 = 6 R 2

32 ÷ 6 = 5 R 2

I am **32**.

7.

$$\overset{+4}{\frown}\ \overset{+4}{\frown}\ \overset{+5}{\frown}\ \overset{+5}{\frown}\ \overset{+4}{\frown}\ \overset{+4}{\frown}\ \overset{+5}{\frown}\ \overset{+5}{\frown}\ \overset{+4}{\frown}\ \overset{+4}{\frown}\ \overset{+5}{\frown}$$

2, 6, 10, 15, 20, 24, **28**, **33**, 38, 42, **46**, 51

8.

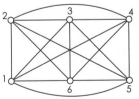

1st person exchanged handshakes with 5 other people.

2nd person exchanged handshakes with 4 other people.

3rd person exchanged handshakes with 3 other people.

4th person exchanged handshakes with 2 other people.

5th person exchanged handshakes with 1 other person.

5 + 4 + 3 + 2 + 1 = 15

15 handshakes were exchanged.

9. When shared by 3 boys, the number of peaches could be 4, 7, 10, (13), 16, or 19.
When shared by 4 boys, the number of peaches could be 5, 9, (13), or 17.

13 ÷ 3 = 4 R 1

13 ÷ 4 = 3 R 1

There are **13** peaches in the bag.

10. A = C

B – A = 1

A + B + C = 4

Using the guess-and-check method:

2 – 1 = 1

1 + 2 + 1 = 4

The 3-digit odd number is **121**.

11. 44 – 32 = 12

56 – 44 = 12

68 – 56 = 12

68 + 12 = 80

10 workers need **80** days to build the same building.

12. 3 × 7 = 21

21 × 5 = 105

The sum of the facing page numbers is 105.

52 + 53 = 105

The facing page numbers are **52** and **53**.

Singapore Math Level 3A & 3B

Unit 10: Money

1. **8.35**
$5 + $3 = $8
$8 + 35¢ = $8.35

2. **51.20**
$43 + $8 = $51
$51 + 20¢ = $51.20

3. **104.75**
$14 + $90 = $104
$104 + 75¢ = $104.75

4. **98.90**
$30 + $68 = $98
$98 + 90¢ = $98.90

5. **9.60**
5¢ + 55¢ = 60¢
$9 + 60¢ = $9.60

6. **24.90**
$24 + 90¢ = $24.90

7. **70.80**
$70 + 80¢ = $70.80

8. **89.20**
20¢ + $6.80 = $7
$82.20 + $7 = $89.20

9. **55.85**
$53 + $2 = $55
60¢ + 25¢ = 85¢
$55 + 85¢ = $55.85

10. **45.30**
20¢ + $1.80 = $2
$43.30 + $2 = $45.30

11. **18.20, 1.00**
19.20, 30
18.90

12. **26.90, 1.00**
27.90, 20
27.70

13. **72.50, 1.00**
73.50, 10
73.40

14. **59.60, 1.00**
60.60, 20
60.40

15. **76.40, 1.00**
77.40, 30
77.10

16.
$23.50
+ $13.20
$36.70

17.
$ 1 1 1
$ 86.75
+ $ 37.45
$124.20

18.
$ 1   1
$515.55
+ $ 79.25
$594.80

19.
$ 1
$4.35
+ $0.90
$5.25

20.
$ 1
$73.20
+ $18.00
$91.20

21.
$ 1 1
$125.80
+ $214.40
$340.20

22.
$217.00
+ $142.85
$359.85

23.
$ 1
$ 56.20
+ $ 64.15
$120.35

24.
$ 1 1
$49.70
+ $28.50
$78.20

25.
$ 1 1
$67.90
+ $17.70
$85.60

26. **34.40**
$39 – $5 = $34
$34 + 40¢ = $34.40

27. **74.55**
$78 – $4 = $74
$74 + 55¢ = $74.55

28. **36.10**
70¢ – 60¢ = 10¢
$36 + 10¢ = $36.10

29. **82.55**
75¢ – 20¢ = 55¢
$82 + 55¢ = $82.55

30. **48.15**
60¢ – 45¢ = 15¢
$48 + 15¢ = $48.15

31. **99.15**
50¢ – 35¢ = 15¢
$99 + 15¢ = $99.15

32. **83.20**
30¢ – 10¢ = 20¢
$87 – $4 = $83
$83 + 20¢ = $83.20

33. **66.20**
55¢ – 35¢ = 20¢
$69 – $3 = $66
$66 + 20¢ = $66.20

34. **91.30**
60¢ – 30¢ = 30¢
$92 – $1 = $91
$91 + 30¢ = $91.30

35. **51.30**
80¢ – 50¢ = 30¢
$58 – $7 = $51
$51 + 30¢ = $51.30

36. **67.40, 1.00**
66.40, 20
66.60

37. **46.20, 1.00**
45.20, 30
45.50

38. **28.30, 1.00**
27.30, 10
27.40

39. **70.60, 1.00**
69.60, 20
69.80

40. **45.20, 1.00**
44.20, 10
44.30

41.
$7.80
– $3.50
$4.30

42.
$50.00
– $ 5.60
$44.40

43.
$280.50
– $ 66.60
$213.90

44.
$23.10
– $ 2.30
$20.80

45.
$758.70
– $329.40
$429.30

46.
$143.05
– $ 21.80
$121.25

47.
$955.60
– $ 89.45
$866.15

48.
$49.25
– $ 5.60
$43.65

49.
$10.00
– $ 3.45
$ 6.55

50.
$659.20
– $ 92.25
$566.95

51. (a) **8.80**
$3.20 + $5.60 = $8.80

(b) **12.95**
$5.60 + $7.35 = $12.95

(c) **kite and a box of crayons**
$1.15 + $3.20 = $4.35

(d) **7.40**
$11.45 + $1.15 = $12.60
$20 – $12.60 = $7.40

(e) **3.25**
$7.35 – $4.10 = $3.25

52.

$1.10	$3.50

?

$1.10 + $3.50 = $4.60
Ashley pays **$4.60** altogether.

53.

$75.35	?

$100

$100 – $75.35 = $24.65
She would receive **$24.65** in change.

54.

Desmond | $500 |
Brother | ? | $200 | ?

$500 + $200 = $700
$700 + $500 = $1,200
His parents received **$1,200** altogether.

55.

| $75.70 | $125 | $360 |
?

$75.70 + $125 = $200.70
$200.70 + $360.00 = $560.70
She spends **$560.70** altogether every month.

56.

$750
| $200 | | | | |
?

$750 – $200 = $550
The chairs cost **$550**.

57.

| $500 | $350 | ? |
$1,000

$500 + $350 = $850
$1,000 – $850 = $150
Beth had to save **$150** in March.

58.

| $34.90 | ? |
$40.00

4 × $10.00 = $40.00
$40.00 – $34.90 = $5.10
She should receive **$5.10** in change.

59. (a)

| $19.65 | $43.60 |
?

$19.65 + $43.60 = $63.25
Aaron had **$63.25** at first.

(b)

Andy | $80.35 | $19.65 |
Aaron | $63.25 | ?

$80.35 + $19.65 = $100.00
$100.00 – $63.25 = $36.75
Andy had **$36.75** more than Aaron.

Unit 11: Length, Mass, and Volume

1. **3, 23**
   300 cm + 23 cm = 3 m 23 cm
2. **7, 10**
   700 cm + 10 cm = 7 m 10 cm
3. **8, 5**
   800 cm + 5 cm = 8 m 5 cm
4. **10, 0**
   1,000 cm = 10 m
5. **15, 25**
   1,500 cm + 25 cm = 15 m 25 cm
6. **5, 21**
   500 cm + 21 cm = 5 m 21 cm
7. **6, 6**
   600 cm + 6 cm = 6 m 6 cm

8. **21, 56**
   2,100 cm + 56 cm = 21 m 56 cm
9. **0, 43**
10. **23, 36**
    2,300 cm + 36 cm = 23 m 36 cm
11. **434**
    400 cm + 34 cm = 434 cm
12. **110**
    100 cm + 10 cm = 110 cm
13. **1,005**
    1,000 cm + 5 cm = 1,005 cm
14. **656**
    600 cm + 56 cm = 656 cm
15. **2,000**
    20 × 100 = 2,000 cm
16. **808**
    800 cm + 8 cm = 808 cm
17. **1,530**
    1,500 cm + 30 cm = 1,530 cm
18. **789**
    700 cm + 89 cm = 789 cm
19. **3,140**
    3,100 cm + 40 cm = 3,140 cm
20. **945**
    900 cm + 45 cm = 945 cm
21. **1, 456**
    1,000 m + 456 m = 1 km 456 m
22. **6, 830**
    6,000 m + 830 m = 6 km 830 m
23. **1, 0**
    1,000 m = 1 km
24. **6, 592**
    6,000 m + 592 m = 6 km 592 m
25. **9, 225**
    9,000 m + 225 m = 9 km 225 m
26. **4, 50**
    4,000 m + 50 m = 4 km 50 m
27. **8, 3**
    8,000 m + 3 m = 8 km 3 m
28. **2, 6**
    2,000 m + 6 m = 2 km 6 m
29. **3, 100**
    3,000 m + 100 m = 3 km 100 m
30. **7, 707**
    7,000 m + 707 m = 7 km 707 m
31. **3,850**
    3,000 m + 850 m = 3,850 m
32. **1,070**
    1,000 m + 70 m = 1,070 m
33. **5,000**
    5 × 1,000 = 5,000 m
34. **9,220**
    9,000 m + 220 m = 9,220 m
35. **12,500**
    12,000 m + 500 m = 12,500 m
36. **27,003**
    27,000 m + 3 m = 27,003 m
37. **9,090**
    9,000 m + 90 m = 9,090 m
38. **20,100**
    20,000 m + 100 m = 20,100 m
39. **2,300**
    2,000 m + 300 m = 2,300 m

Singapore Math Level 3A & 3B

40. **1,309**
$1,000 m + 309 m = 1,309 m$

41. (a) **2,700, 2, 700**   (c) **1,500, 1, 500**
(b) **2,350, 2, 350**   (d) **1,070, 1, 70**

42. **km**
43. **cm**
44. **cm**
45. **m**
46. **1,000**
$1 × 1,000 = 1,000 g$
47. **1,238**
$1,000 g + 238 g = 1,238 g$
48. **3,300**
$3,000 g + 300 g = 3,300 g$
49. **9,569**
$9,000 g + 569 g = 9,569 g$
50. **5,955**
$5,000 g + 955 g = 5,955 g$
51. **7,067**
$7,000 g + 67 g = 7,067 g$
52. **10,760**
$10,000 g + 760 g = 10,760 g$
53. **4,008**
$4,000 g + 8 g = 4,008 g$
54. **8,642**
$8,000 g + 642 g = 8,642 g$
55. **2,484**
$2,000 g + 484 g = 2,484 g$
56. **1, 369**
$1,000 g + 369 g = 1 kg 369 g$
57. **4, 820**
$4,000 g + 820 g = 4 kg 820 g$
58. **12, 790**
$12,000 g + 790 g = 12 kg 790 g$
59. **6, 606**
$6,000 g + 606 g = 6 kg 606 g$
60. **10, 1**
$10,000 g + 1 g = 10 kg 1 g$
61. **3, 33**
$3000 g + 33 g = 3 kg 33 g$
62. **5, 115**
$5,000 g + 115 g = 5 kg 115 g$
63. **8, 780**
$8,000 g + 780 g = 8 kg 780 g$
64. **2, 200**
$2,000 g + 200 g = 2 kg 200 g$
65. **9, 90**
$9,000 g + 90 g = 9 kg 90 g$
66. **600**
67. **1,800**
68. **2,500**
69. **660**
70. **2,600**
71. **150**
72. **g**
73. **kg**
74. **kg**
75. **g**
76. **300**
77. **750**
$500 mL + 250 mL = 750 mL$
78. **1, 300**
$1 L + 300 mL = 1 L 300 mL$

79. **2, 70**
$1 L + 1 L + 70 mL = 2 L 70 mL$
80. **350**
$100 mL + 100 mL + 150 mL = 350 mL$
81. **1, 590**
$1 L + 500 mL + 90 mL = 1 L 590 mL$
82. **1,000**
$1 × 1,000 = 1,000 mL$
83. **4,368**
$4,000 mL + 368 mL = 4,368 mL$
84. **10,010**
$10,000 mL + 10 mL = 10,010 mL$
85. **8,818**
$8,000 mL + 818 mL = 8,818 mL$
86. **12,200**
$12,000 mL + 200 mL = 12,200 mL$
87. **3,008**
$3,000 mL + 8 mL = 3,008 mL$
88. **8,096**
$8,000 mL + 96 mL = 8,096 mL$
89. **7,478**
$7,000 mL + 478 mL = 7,478 mL$
90. **9,009**
$9,000 mL + 9 mL = 9,009 mL$
91. **11,110**
$11,000 mL + 110 mL = 11,110 mL$
92. **4, 352**
$4,000 mL + 352 mL = 4 L 352 mL$
93. **9, 909**
$9,000 mL + 909 mL = 9 L 909 mL$
94. **3, 100**
$3,000 mL + 100 mL = 3 L 100 mL$
95. **8, 702**
$8,000 mL + 702 mL = 8 L 702 mL$
96. **2, 0**
$2,000 mL + 0 mL = 2 L 0 mL$
97. **5, 15**
$5,000 mL + 15 mL = 5 L 15 mL$
98. **7, 7**
$7,000 mL + 7 mL = 7 L 7 mL$
99. **6, 60**
$6,000 mL + 60 mL = 6 L 60 mL$
100. **10, 1**
$10,000 mL + 1 mL = 10 L 1 mL$
101. **1, 100**
$1,000 mL + 100 mL = 1 L 100 mL$
102. **mL**
103. **L**
104. **mL**
105. **L**

Unit 12: Problem Solving (Length, Mass, and Volume)

1.
$325 - 88 = 237$
The length of the wooden plank is **237 cm**.

2.
$840 ÷ 5 = 168$

Singapore Math Level 3A & 3B

The length of each piece of ribbon is **168 cm**.

3.
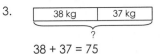
38 kg	37 kg

?

$38 + 37 = 75$
Their total mass is **75 kg**.

$$\begin{array}{r} {}^1 3\,8 \\ +\ 3\,7 \\ \hline 7\,5 \end{array}$$

4.
?	900 g

3,000 g

$3,000 - 900 = 2100$
$2,100\ g = 2,000\ g + 100\ g = 2\ kg\ 100\ g$
She used **2 kg 100 g** of flour.

$$\begin{array}{r} {}^{2}\,{}^{10}3,\!0\,0\,0 \\ -\ \ \ 9\,0\,0 \\ \hline 2,\!1\,0\,0 \end{array}$$

5.
7,900 mL	?

10,360 mL

$10,360 - 7,900 = 2,460$
She adds **2,460 mL** of milk.

$$\begin{array}{r} {}^{0}\,{}^{9}\,{}^{13}1\,0,\!3\,6\,0 \\ -\ \ \ 7,\!9\,0\,0 \\ \hline 2,\!4\,6\,0 \end{array}$$

6.
?	18 L

40 L

$40 - 18 = 22$
She has used up **22 L** of gasoline.

$$\begin{array}{r} {}^{3}\,{}^{10}4\,0 \\ -\ 1\,8 \\ \hline 2\,2 \end{array}$$

7.
?	?	?

1,800 g

$1,800 \div 3 = 600$
The mass of each box of crackers was **600 g**.

8.
550 mL	550 mL	550 mL	550 mL	550 mL	550 mL	550 mL	550 mL	550 mL	550 mL	550 mL	550 mL

?

$550 \times 12 = 6,600$
$6,600\ mL = 6,000\ mL + 600\ mL$
$ = 6\ L\ 600\ mL$
She bought **6 L 600 mL** of orange juice.

$$\begin{array}{r} {}^{1}\,5\,5\,0 \\ \times\ \ \ 1\,2 \\ \hline 4,\!1\,0\,0 \\ 5\,5\,0 \\ \hline 6,\!6\,0\,0 \end{array}$$

9.
272 cm
	?

555 cm

$555 - 272 = 283$
$283\ cm = 200\ cm + 83\ cm = 2\ m\ 83\ cm$
The length of the third stick is **2 m 83 cm**.

$$\begin{array}{r} {}^{4}\,{}^{15}5\,5\,5 \\ -\ 2\,7\,2 \\ \hline 2\,8\,3 \end{array}$$

10.
table | 3,960 g |
chair | 2,700 g | ?

$3,960 - 2,700 = 1,260$
The table is **1,260 g** heavier than the chair.

$$\begin{array}{r} 3,\!9\,6\,0 \\ -\ 2,\!7\,0\,0 \\ \hline 1,\!2\,6\,0 \end{array}$$

11. $8 + 6 + 8 + 6 = 28$
The fence will be **28 m** long.

8 m
6 m

12.
Basir | 4,870 g | } ?
Andy | ? | 3,560 g

$4,870 - 3,560 = 1,310$
Andy's bag of groceries is 1,310 g.
$4,870 + 1,310 = 6,180$
$6,180\ g = 6,000\ g + 180\ g = 6\ kg\ 180\ g$
Andy and Basir's bags of groceries are **6 kg 180 g**.

$$\begin{array}{r} 4,\!8\,7\,0 \\ -\ 3,\!5\,6\,0 \\ \hline 1,\!3\,1\,0 \end{array}$$

$$\begin{array}{r} {}^{1}4,\!8\,7\,0 \\ +\ 1,\!3\,1\,0 \\ \hline 6,\!1\,8\,0 \end{array}$$

13.
30,960 g	10,040 g

?

$30,960 + 10,040 = 41,000$

$$\begin{array}{r} 3\,0,\!9\,6\,0 \\ +\ 1\,0,\!0\,4\,0 \\ \hline 4\,1,\!0\,0\,0 \end{array}$$

$41,000\ g = 41\ kg$
It sold **41 kg** of fish on both days.

14.
Sam | 8,300 mL | } ?
Evan | ? | 6,970 mL

$8,300 - 6,970 = 1,330$
Evan bought 1,330 mL of paint.
$8,300 + 1,330 = 9,630$
They bought **9,630 mL** of paint altogether.

$$\begin{array}{r} {}^{7}\,{}^{12}\,{}^{10}8,\!3\,0\,0 \\ -\ 6,\!9\,7\,0 \\ \hline 1,\!3\,3\,0 \end{array}$$

$$\begin{array}{r} 8,\!3\,0\,0 \\ +\ 1,\!3\,3\,0 \\ \hline 9,\!6\,3\,0 \end{array}$$

15.
Kelly | 125 g |
Sister | | | | | ?

$125 \times 4 = 500$
Her sister used **500 g** more flour than Kelly.

$$\begin{array}{r} {}^{1}\,{}^{2}1\,2\,5 \\ \times\ \ \ \ 4 \\ \hline 5\,0\,0 \end{array}$$

16.
A | 135 cm |
B | | | | } ?

$135 \times 4 = 540$
The total height of both trees is **540 cm**.

$$\begin{array}{r} {}^{1}\,{}^{2}1\,3\,5 \\ \times\ \ \ \ 4 \\ \hline 5\,4\,0 \end{array}$$

17. Andre: $15\ m \times 3\ m = 45\ m^2$
Tim: $\ \ \ 12\ m \times 4\ m = 48\ m^2$
(a) **Tim** has to paint more wall space.
(b) $48 - 45 = 3$
He has to paint **3 m²** more wall space.

18.
?
1 km 400 m	800 m	1 km 10 m

$1\ km\ 400\ m + 800\ m + 1\ km\ 10\ m = 3\ km\ 210\ m$
Margaret walked a total distance of **3 km 210 m**.

19.
Jake | 6,500 mL | 2,765 mL |
Brother | ? | } ?

$6,500 + 2,765 = 9,265$
His brother uses 9,265 mL of water.
$9,265 + 6,500 = 15,765$
$15,765\ mL = 15,000\ mL + 765\ mL$
$ = 15\ L\ 765\ mL$
Both of them use **15 L 765 mL** of water.

$$\begin{array}{r} {}^{1}6,\!5\,0\,0 \\ +\ 2,\!7\,6\,5 \\ \hline 9,\!2\,6\,5 \end{array}$$

$$\begin{array}{r} 9,\!2\,6\,5 \\ +\ 6,\!5\,0\,0 \\ \hline 1\,5,\!7\,6\,5 \end{array}$$

20.
420 mL	420 mL	420 mL	420 mL	420 mL	420 mL	420 mL	420 mL

?

(a) $420 \times 8 = 3,360$
The total volume of 8 glasses of milk was **3,360 mL**.

(b) $3,360 + 250 = 3,610$
$3,610\ mL = 3,000\ mL + 610\ mL$
$ = 3\ L\ 610\ mL$
There was **3 L 610 mL** of milk in all.

$$\begin{array}{r} {}^{1}4\,2\,0 \\ \times\ \ \ \ 8 \\ \hline 3,\!3\,6\,0 \end{array}$$

$$\begin{array}{r} 3,\!3\,6\,0 \\ +\ \ \ 2\,5\,0 \\ \hline 3,\!6\,1\,0 \end{array}$$

21.
2 L		2 L

14 L

(a) $14 \div 2 = 7$
He could fill **7** pots of coffee.
(b) $7 - 2 = 5$
5 pots of coffee were used.

Review 5

1. (a) **4, 15**
$415\ cm = 400\ cm + 15\ cm = 4\ m\ 15\ cm$
(b) **8, 30**
$830\ cm = 800\ cm + 30\ cm = 8\ m\ 30\ cm$

2. (a) **6, 269**
   6,269 m = 6,000 m + 269 m = 6 km 269 m
   (b) **5, 500**
   5,500 m = 5,000 m + 500 m = 5 km 500 m
3. (a) **7, 670**
   7,670 g = 7,000 g + 670 g = 7 kg 670 g
   (b) **4, 8**
   4,008 g = 4,000 g + 8 g = 4 kg 8 g
4. (a) **4, 835**
   4,835 mL = 4,000 mL + 835 mL = 4 L 835 mL
   (b) **6, 505**
   6,505 mL = 6,000 mL + 505 mL = 6 L 505 mL
5. (a) **6,975**
   6,000 m + 975 m = 6,975 m
   (b) **8,008**
   8,000 m + 8 m = 8,008 m
6. (a) **905**
   900 cm + 5 cm = 905 cm
   (b) **1,000**
   10 × 100 = 1,000 cm
7. (a) **2,002**
   2,000 mL + 2 mL = 2,002 mL
   (b) **5,275**
   5,000 mL + 275 mL = 5,275 mL
8. (a) **2,636**
   2,000 g + 636 g = 2,636 g
   (b) **5,030**
   5,000 g + 30 g = 5,030 g
9. **2,000**
   2 kg = 2,000 g
10. 1 L + 500 mL + 70 mL = 1 L 570 mL = 1,000 mL + 570 mL
    = **1,570** mL
11. (a) **3.20**
    $1.50 + $1.70 = $3.20
    (b) **3.40**
    2 × $0.80 = $1.60
    $5.00 − $1.60 = $ 3.40
    (c) **40.55**
    4 × $10 = $40
    $40 + $0.55 = $40.55
12. (a) **850**
    (b) **1,400**
    1 km 400 m = 1,000 m + 400 m = 1,400 m
    (c) **1,175**
    1 km 175 m = 1,000 m + 175 m = 1,175 m
13.
   $1,200

   | $500 | $375 | ? |

   $500 + $375 = $875
   $1,200 − $875 = $325
   Ken saves **$325**.

   ```
     $ 5 0 0
   + $ 3 7 5
     $ 8 7 5

      0 11 9 10
   $  1, 2 0 0
   − $    8 7 5
   $      3 2 5
   ```
14.
   | 8 km 120 m | 8 km 120 m |
   ?

   8 km 120 m + 8 km 120 m = 16 km 240 m
   Benjamin jogs **16 km 240 m** daily.
15.
   Alex | $410 |
   Sam | | $75 |
   John | | $160 |
   ?

   $410 − $75 = $335
   $335 + $160 = $495
   John spends **$495**.

   ```
      3 10 10
   $  4  1  0
   − $    7  5
   $    3 3 5

   $    3 3 5
   + $    1 6 0
   $    4 9 5
   ```
16.
   cement | 4 kg 360 g |
   sand | 2 kg 500 g | } ?

   (a) 4 kg 360 g − 2 kg 500 g = 1 kg 860 g
   He mixes **1 kg 860 g** more cement.
   (b) 4 kg 360 g + 2 kg 500 g = 6 kg 860 g
   The total mass of the mixture is
   6 kg 860 g.

   ```
     3 13
   4, 3 6 0
   − 2, 5 0 0
     1, 8 6 0

     4, 3 6 0
   + 2, 5 0 0
     6, 8 6 0
   ```
17.
   5 m 70 cm

   | 2 m 25 cm | ? |

   (a) 5 m 70 cm − 2 m 25 cm = 3 m 45 cm
   Pole B is longer.
   (b) 3 m 45 cm − 2 m 25 cm = 1 m 20 cm
   Pole B is **120 cm** longer than Pole A.

   ```
       6 10
     5 7 0
   − 2 2 5
     3 4 5

     3 4 5
   − 2 2 5
     1 2 0
   ```
18.
   | 250 mL | 250 mL | 250 mL | 250 mL |
   ?

   250 × 4 = 1,000
   1,000 mL = 1 L
   The total volume of the four cartons of milk is **1 L**.

   ```
       2
       2 5 0
   ×       4
     1, 0 0 0
   ```
19.
   | $3.60 | $3.55 | ? |
   $10.00

   $3.60 + $3.55 = $7.15
   $10.00 − $7.15 = $2.85
   The oranges cost **$2.85**.

   ```
        1
     $ 3. 6 0
   + $ 3. 5 5
     $ 7. 1 5

     0 9  9 10
   $ 1 0. 0 0
   − $   7. 1 5
   $     2. 8 5
   ```
20.
   | ? | ? | ? | ? | ? | ? |
   3 L 250 mL + 1,670 mL

   3,250 + 1,670 = 4,920
   4,920 ÷ 6 = 820
   There was **820 mL** of orange juice
   in each container.

   ```
     3, 2 5 0
   + 1, 6 7 0
     4, 9 2 0

          8 2 0
   6 ) 4, 9 2 0
        4 8
          1 2
          1 2
            0
            0
            0
   ```

Unit 13: Bar Graphs

1.

2.

248

Singapore Math Level 3A & 3B

3.

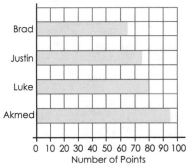

Number of Points

4.

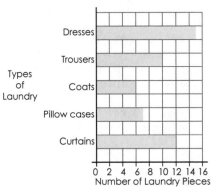

Types of Laundry

Number of Laundry Pieces

5. (a) **28**
   (b) **bananas**
   (c) **oranges**
   (d) $36 - 16 = $ **20**
   (e) $28 - 20 = $ **8**
   (f) $16 + 28 + 36 + 20 = $ **100**

6. (a) **20**
   (b) $16 - 14 = $ **2**
   (c) $20 - 8 = $ **12**
   (d) **dragonflies**
   (e) **birds**
   (f) $14 + 2 + 20 + 8 + 16 = $ **60**

7. (a) **45**
   (b) $40 - 15 = $ **25**
   (c) **Thursday**
      $35¢ ÷ 7 = 5¢$
   (d) **1.60**
      $15¢ + 40¢ + 20¢ + 5¢ + 45¢ + 35¢ = 160¢ = \$1.60$
   (e) **8.40**
      $\$10.00 - \$1.60 = \$8.40$

8. (a) **6**
   (b) **10**
   (c) $18 - 4 = $ **14**
   (d) $18 - 12 = $ **6**
   (e) $12 + 6 + 18 + 4 + 10 = $ **50**

Unit 14: Fractions

1. **8**
2. **10**
3. **1**
4. **5**
5. **5**
6. $\frac{2}{6}$
7. $\frac{4}{8}$
8. $\frac{6}{8}$
9. $\frac{16}{24}$
10. $\frac{8}{20}$
11. $2 \times 3 = $ **6**
12. $8 \times 5 = $ **40**
13. $3 \times 4 = $ **12**

14. $10 \times 8 = $ **80**
15. $9 \times 7 = $ **63**
16. $4 \times 4 = $ **16**
17. $7 \times 3 = $ **21**
18. $2 \times 6 = $ **12**
19. $11 \times 7 = $ **77**
20. $3 \times 6 = $ **18**
21. **2, 15, 20, 25**
    $1 \times 2 = 2$
    $5 \times 3 = 15$
    $5 \times 4 = 20$
    $5 \times 5 = 25$
22. **6, 9, 32, 40**
    $3 \times 2 = 6$
    $3 \times 3 = 9$
    $8 \times 4 = 32$
    $8 \times 5 = 40$
23. **10, 6, 20, 25**
    $5 \times 2 = 10$
    $2 \times 3 = 6$
    $5 \times 4 = 20$
    $5 \times 5 = 25$
24. **8, 3, 16, 20**
    $4 \times 2 = 8$
    $1 \times 3 = 3$
    $4 \times 4 = 16$
    $4 \times 5 = 20$
25. **2, 3, 28, 35**
    $1 \times 2 = 2$
    $1 \times 3 = 3$
    $7 \times 4 = 28$
    $7 \times 5 = 35$
26. $\frac{7 ÷ 7}{21 ÷ 7} = \frac{1}{3}$
27. $\frac{3 ÷ 3}{9 ÷ 3} = \frac{1}{3}$
28. $\frac{8 ÷ 8}{16 ÷ 8} = \frac{1}{2}$
29. $\frac{36 ÷ 9}{45 ÷ 9} = \frac{4}{5}$
30. $\frac{35 ÷ 7}{42 ÷ 7} = \frac{5}{6}$
31. $\frac{9 ÷ 9}{63 ÷ 9} = \frac{1}{7}$
32. $\frac{44 ÷ 22}{66 ÷ 22} = \frac{2}{3}$
33. $\frac{64 ÷ 8}{72 ÷ 8} = \frac{8}{9}$
34. $\frac{12 ÷ 6}{18 ÷ 6} = \frac{2}{3}$
35. $\frac{9 ÷ 3}{24 ÷ 3} = \frac{3}{8}$
36. $\frac{3}{6}, \frac{2}{6}$
37. $\frac{4}{10}, \frac{5}{10}$
38. $\frac{4}{8}, \frac{5}{8}$
39. $\frac{7}{12}, \frac{6}{12}$
40. $\frac{3}{4}, \frac{2}{4}$
41. $\frac{1}{6}$
42. $\frac{2}{9}$

43. $\frac{3}{9}$
44. $\frac{5}{11}$
45. $\frac{7}{12}$
46. $\frac{2}{3}$
    $\frac{2 \times 4}{3 \times 4} = \frac{8}{12}$
47. $\frac{2}{5}$
    $\frac{3 \times 5}{8 \times 5} = \frac{15}{40}$
    $\frac{2 \times 8}{5 \times 8} = \frac{16}{40}$
48. $\frac{4}{6}$
    $\frac{2 \times 2}{8 \times 2} = \frac{4}{16}$
49. $\frac{2}{7}$
    $\frac{1 \times 2}{9 \times 2} = \frac{2}{18}$
50. $\frac{3}{11}$
    $\frac{1 \times 3}{4 \times 3} = \frac{3}{12}$
51. $\frac{8}{9}, \frac{5}{9}, \frac{3}{9}$
52. $\frac{3}{4}, \frac{4}{6}, \frac{2}{8}$
    $\frac{4 \times 4}{6 \times 4} = \frac{16}{24}$
    $\frac{2 \times 3}{8 \times 3} = \frac{6}{24}$
    $\frac{3 \times 6}{4 \times 6} = \frac{18}{24}$
53. $\frac{3}{4}, \frac{7}{12}, \frac{1}{6}$
    $\frac{3 \times 3}{4 \times 3} = \frac{9}{12}$
    $\frac{1 \times 2}{6 \times 2} = \frac{2}{12}$
54. $\frac{8}{9}, \frac{2}{5}, \frac{4}{15}$
    $\frac{2 \times 4}{5 \times 4} = \frac{8}{20}$
    $\frac{4 ÷ 2}{15 ÷ 2} = \frac{8}{30}$
55. $\frac{6}{7}, \frac{6}{9}, \frac{6}{12}$
56. $\frac{2}{5}, \frac{2}{4}, \frac{2}{3}$
57. $\frac{1}{4}, \frac{3}{8}, \frac{4}{6}$
    $\frac{3 \times 3}{8 \times 3} = \frac{9}{24}$
    $\frac{4 \times 4}{6 \times 4} = \frac{16}{24}$
    $\frac{1 \times 6}{4 \times 6} = \frac{6}{24}$
58. $\frac{1}{5}, \frac{3}{6}, \frac{6}{10}$
    $\frac{3 \times 2}{6 \times 2} = \frac{6}{12}$
    $\frac{1 \times 6}{5 \times 6} = \frac{6}{30}$

Singapore Math Level 3A & 3B

59. $\dfrac{11}{20}, \dfrac{12}{20}, \dfrac{18}{20}$

60. $\dfrac{4}{7}, \dfrac{2}{3}, \dfrac{5}{6}$

$\dfrac{4^{\times 5}}{7^{\times 5}} = \dfrac{20}{35}$

$\dfrac{5^{\times 4}}{6^{\times 4}} = \dfrac{20}{24}$

$\dfrac{2^{\times 10}}{3^{\times 10}} = \dfrac{20}{30}$

61. $\dfrac{2^{\times 3}}{3^{\times 3}} + \dfrac{1}{9} = \dfrac{6}{9} + \dfrac{1}{9} = \dfrac{7}{9}$

62. $\dfrac{1}{4} + \dfrac{1^{\times 2}}{2^{\times 2}} = \dfrac{1}{4} + \dfrac{2}{4} = \dfrac{3}{4}$

63. $\dfrac{5}{12} + \dfrac{1^{\times 2}}{6^{\times 2}} = \dfrac{5}{12} + \dfrac{2}{12} = \dfrac{7}{12}$

64. $\dfrac{2^{\times 2}}{5^{\times 2}} + \dfrac{3}{10} = \dfrac{4}{10} + \dfrac{3}{10} = \dfrac{7}{10}$

65. $\dfrac{3}{8} + \dfrac{1^{\times 2}}{4^{\times 2}} = \dfrac{3}{8} + \dfrac{2}{8} = \dfrac{5}{8}$

66. $\dfrac{1^{\times 5}}{2^{\times 5}} - \dfrac{1^{\times 2}}{5^{\times 2}} = \dfrac{5}{10} - \dfrac{2}{10} = \dfrac{3}{10}$

67. $\dfrac{4^{\times 2}}{5^{\times 2}} - \dfrac{7}{10} = \dfrac{8}{10} - \dfrac{7}{10} = \dfrac{1}{10}$

68. $\dfrac{7}{8} - \dfrac{3^{\times 2}}{4^{\times 2}} = \dfrac{7}{8} - \dfrac{6}{8} = \dfrac{1}{8}$

69. $\dfrac{5^{\times 2}}{6^{\times 2}} - \dfrac{5}{12} = \dfrac{10}{12} - \dfrac{5}{12} = \dfrac{5}{12}$

70. $\dfrac{4}{9} - \dfrac{1^{\times 3}}{3^{\times 3}} = \dfrac{4}{9} - \dfrac{3}{9} = \dfrac{1}{9}$

71. $\dfrac{1}{9} + \dfrac{1^{\times 3}}{3^{\times 3}} + \dfrac{4}{9} = \dfrac{1}{9} + \dfrac{3}{9} + \dfrac{4}{9} = \dfrac{8}{9}$

72. $\dfrac{1^{\times 2}}{4^{\times 2}} + \dfrac{3}{8} + \dfrac{1}{8} = \dfrac{2}{8} + \dfrac{3}{8} + \dfrac{1}{8} = \dfrac{6}{8}$

73. $1 - \dfrac{7}{12} - \dfrac{1^{\times 2}}{6^{\times 2}} = \dfrac{12}{12} - \dfrac{7}{12} - \dfrac{2}{12} = \dfrac{3}{12}$

74. $1 - \dfrac{1^{\times 3}}{3^{\times 3}} - \dfrac{5}{9} = \dfrac{9}{9} - \dfrac{3}{9} - \dfrac{5}{9} = \dfrac{1}{9}$

75. $\dfrac{3}{10} + \dfrac{1^{\times 5}}{2^{\times 5}} + \dfrac{1}{10} = \dfrac{3}{10} + \dfrac{5}{10} + \dfrac{1}{10} = \dfrac{9}{10}$

76. $\dfrac{2}{6} + \dfrac{1^{\times 2}}{3^{\times 2}} + \dfrac{1}{6} = \dfrac{2}{6} + \dfrac{2}{6} + \dfrac{1}{6} = \dfrac{5}{6}$

77. $1 - \dfrac{3}{8} - \dfrac{1^{\times 4}}{2^{\times 4}} = \dfrac{8}{8} - \dfrac{3}{8} - \dfrac{4}{8} = \dfrac{1}{8}$

78. $1 - \dfrac{3^{\times 2}}{5^{\times 2}} - \dfrac{1}{10} = \dfrac{10}{10} - \dfrac{6}{10} - \dfrac{1}{10} = \dfrac{3}{10}$

Unit 15: Time

1. **1:20, 20 minutes after 1**
2. **5:50, 10 minutes to 6**
3. **10:15, 15 minutes after 10**
4. **3:05, 5 minutes after 3**
5. **6:55, 5 minutes to 7**
6. **9:30, 30 minutes after 9**
7. **7:40, 20 minutes to 8**
8. **25**
9. **19**
10. **4**
11. **7**
12. **5**
13. **22**
14. **6**
15. **10**

16. 3 × 60 min. = **180** min.
17. 60 min. + 20 min. = **80** min.
18. 4 × 60 min. = 240 min.
    240 min. + 5 min. = **245** min.
19. 8 × 60 min. = 480 min.
    480 min. + 15 min. = **495** min.
20. 6 × 60 min. = 360 min.
    360 min. + 30 min. = **390** min.
21. 420 min. ÷ 60 min. = **7** hr.
22. 300 min. ÷ 60 min. = **5** hr.
23. 600 min. ÷ 60 min. = **10** hr.
24. 240 min. ÷ 60 min. = **4** hr.
25. 540 min. ÷ 60 min. = **9** hr.
26. 75 min. = 60 min. + 15 min. = **1** hr. **15** min.
27. 515 min. = 480 min. + 35 min. = **8** hr. **35** min.
28. 455 min. = 420 min. + 35 min. = **7** hr. **35** min.
29. 190 min. = 180 min. + 10 min. = **3** hr. **10** min.
30. 430 min. = 420 min. + 10 min. = **7** hr. **10** min.
31. **5, 50**
    5 min. + 45 min. = 50 min.
    3 hr. + 2 hr. = 5 hr.
32. **10, 55**
    17 min. + 38 min. = 55 min.
    7 hr. + 3 hr. = 10 hr.
33. **3, 58**
    19 min. + 39 min. = 58 min.
    2 hr. + 1 hr. = 3 hr.
34. **8, 9**
    13 min. + 56 min. = 69 min. = 1 hr. 9 min.
    5 hr. + 2 hr. + 1 hr. 9 min. = 8 hr. 9 min.
35. **11, 18**
    28 min. + 50 min. = 78 min. = 1 hr. 18 min.
    6 hr. + 4 hr. + 1 hr. 18 min. = 11 hr. 18 min.
36. **10, 20**
    35 min. + 45 min. = 80 min. = 1 hr. 20 min.
    8 hr. + 1 hr. + 1 hr. 20 min. = 10 hr. 20 min.
37. **2, 20**
    50 min. – 30 min. = 20 min.
    4 hr. – 2 hr. = 2 hr.
38. **3, 10**
    35 min. – 25 min. = 10 min.
    10 hr. – 7 hr. = 3 hr.
39. **5, 25**
    30 min. – 5 min. = 25 min.
    6 hr. – 1 hr. = 5 hr.
40. **4, 45**
    8 hr. 25 min. = 7 hr. 60 min. + 25 min. = 7 hr. 85 min.
    85 min. – 40 min. = 45 min.
    7 hr. – 3 hr. = 4 hr.
41. **3, 30**
    5 hr. 15 min. = 4 hr. 60 min. + 15 min. = 4 hr. 75 min.
    75 min. – 45 min. = 30 min.
    4 hr. – 1 hr. = 3 hr.
42. **5, 30**
    10 hr. 20 min. = 9 hr. 60 min + 20 min. = 9 hr. 80 min.
    80 min. – 50 min. = 30 min.
    9 hr. – 4 hr. = 5 hr.
43. **30**

    |———————— 30 min. ————————|
    4:20 P.M.   4:50 P.M.

44. **2, 15**

    |—— 1 hr. ——|—— 1 hr. ——|—15 min.—|
    2:30 P.M.   3:30 P.M.   4:30 P.M. 4:45 P.M.

250

45. **3, 15**

| 1 hr. | 1 hr. | 1 hr. | 15 min. |
10:25 A.M. 11:25 A.M. 12:25 P.M. 1:25 P.M. 1:40 P.M.

46. **3, 55**

| 1 hr. | 1 hr. | 1 hr. | 20 min. | 35 min. |
11:40 A.M. 12:40 P.M. 1:40 P.M. 2:40 P.M. 3:00 P.M. 3:35 P.M.

47. **3, 45**

| 1 hr. | 1 hr. | 1 hr. | 45 min. |
7:10 P.M. 8:10 P.M. 9:10 P.M. 10:10 P.M. 10:55 P.M.

48. **8**

| 1 hr. | 1 hr. | 1 hr. | 1 hr. | 1 hr. | 1 hr. | 1 hr. | 1 hr. |
11:30 A.M. 12:30 P.M. 1:30 P.M. 2:30 P.M. 3:30 P.M. 4:30 P.M. 5:30 P.M. 6:30 P.M. 7:30 P.M.

49. **4, 40**

| 1 hr. | 1 hr. | 1 hr. | 1 hr. | 40 min. |
1:15 P.M. 2:15 P.M. 3:15 P.M. 4:15 P.M. 5:15 P.M. 5:55 P.M.

50. **7:20 A.M.**

51. **12:10 A.M.**

52. **3:10 A.M.**

53. **4:15 P.M.**

54. **12:30 P.M.**

55.

| 1 hr. | 20 min. |
5:30 P.M. 6:30 P.M. 6:50 P.M.

The movie ended at **6:50 P.M.**

56.

| 1 hr. | 1 hr. | 1 hr. | 1 hr. | 40 min. |
10:15 A.M. 11:15 A.M. 12:15 P.M. 1:15 P.M. 2:15 P.M. 2:55 P.M.

He stayed at his friend's house for **4 hr. 40 min.**

57.

| 55 mins. |
6:05 P.M. 7 P.M.

She must leave her house at **6:05 P.M.**

58. 3 + 2 + 3 + 4 + 2 + 5 = 19 hr.
19 × $125 = $2,375
Matt earns **$2,375** in a week.

59. (a)

| 8 | 8 | 8 | 8 | 8 |
?

5 × 8 = 40
The total number of hours she works in a week is **40 hr.**

(b) 40 × $9 = $360
She earns **$360** in a week.

60. (a)

| 2 | 2 | 2 | 2 | 2 | 2 |
?

6 × 2 = 12
He needs **12 hr.** to proofread a series of six chapters.

(b) 12 × $15 = $180
The total amount of money he will be paid for proofreading the six chapters is **$180.**

Review 6

1. (a) **8**
   (b) **6**
   (c) 16 − 10 = **6**
   (d) 6 − 4 = **2**
   (e) 4 + 10 + 8 + 16 + 6 = **44**

2. $\frac{2 \times 5}{9 \times 5} = \frac{\mathbf{10}}{\mathbf{45}}$

3. $\frac{3 \times 4}{7 \times 4} = \frac{\mathbf{12}}{\mathbf{28}}$

4. $\frac{8 \div 2}{10 \div 2} = \frac{\mathbf{4}}{\mathbf{5}}$

5. $\frac{15 \div 5}{25 \div 5} = \frac{\mathbf{3}}{\mathbf{5}}$

6. 76 min. = 60 min. + 16 min. = **1** hr. **16** min.

7. 4 × 60 min. = 240 min.
   240 min. + 15 min. = **255** min.

8. $\frac{1 \times 2}{4 \times 2} + \frac{2}{8} + \frac{3}{8} = \frac{2}{8} + \frac{2}{8} + \frac{3}{8} = \frac{\mathbf{7}}{\mathbf{8}}$

9. $1 - \frac{1 \times 2}{5 \times 2} - \frac{7}{10} = \frac{10}{10} - \frac{2}{10} - \frac{7}{10} = \frac{\mathbf{1}}{\mathbf{10}}$

10. (a) $\frac{\mathbf{4}}{\mathbf{5}}$
    $\frac{4 \times 2}{5 \times 2} = \frac{8}{10}$
    (b) $\frac{\mathbf{8}}{\mathbf{9}}$
    $\frac{2 \times 3}{3 \times 3} = \frac{6}{9}$

11. (a) $\frac{\mathbf{2}}{\mathbf{7}}$
    (b) $\frac{\mathbf{1}}{\mathbf{4}}$
    $\frac{1 \times 2}{4 \times 2} = \frac{2}{8}$

12. $\frac{\mathbf{2}}{\mathbf{3}}, \frac{\mathbf{3}}{\mathbf{6}}, \frac{\mathbf{1}}{\mathbf{6}}$
    $\frac{2 \times 2}{3 \times 2} = \frac{4}{6}$

13. $\frac{\mathbf{1}}{\mathbf{9}}, \frac{\mathbf{1}}{\mathbf{5}}, \frac{\mathbf{1}}{\mathbf{3}}$

14. **20 minutes**, **7**

15. **8, 5**
    35 min. + 30 min. = 65 min. = 1 hr. 5 min.
    4 hr. + 3 hr. + 1 hr. 5 min. = 8 hr. 5 min.

16. (a)
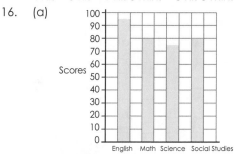

(b) **science**
(c) 80 − 75 = **5**
(d) 95 − 80 = **15**

17. **5, 30**
    9 hr. 15 min. = 8 hr. 60 min. + 15 min.
    = 8 hr. 75 min.
    75 min. − 45 min. = 30 min.
    8 hr. − 3 hr. = 5 hr.

18.

19.

20.

| 1 hr. | 1 hr. | 25 min. |
3:15 P.M. 4:15 P.M. 5:15 P.M. 5:40 P.M.

She left the library at **5:40 P.M.**

Unit 16: Angles

1.

2.

3.

4.

5.

6.

7.

8.

9.

10.

11.

Possible answers for questions 12 to 21:

12.

13.

14.

15.

16.

17.

18.

19.

20.

21.

22. **3, 3**
23. **4, 4**

24. **8, 8**
25. **4, 4**
26. **6, 6**
27.

28.

29.

30.

31.

32. (a) **a, c**
    (b) **d, e**
    (c) **b, f**
33. (a) **b**
    (b) **a**
    (c) **a**
    (d) **a, c, b**
34. (a) **b**
    (b) **a**
    (c) **a**
    (d) **a, c, b**
35. **6, 3**
37. **8, 3**
36. **8, 3**
38. **7, 2**

Unit 17: Perpendicular and Parallel Lines

1. ✓
2. ✓
3. ✗
4. ✓
5. ✗
6. **DC, AB**
   HG, AB
7. **AB, CD**
   KJ, BA
   LM, NO
8. **BC ⊥ CD, ED ⊥ CD,**
   DE ⊥ FE, GF ⊥ FE
9. **AB ⊥ BC, HG ⊥ GF,**
   DC ⊥ CB, EF ⊥ FG,
   CD ⊥ DE, FE ⊥ ED,
   BA ⊥ AH, GH ⊥ HA
10.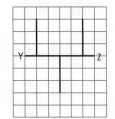

11.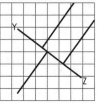

12.

13. ✓
14. ✗
15. ✗
16. ✓
17. ✓
18. **CD // AF, CB // DE,**
    BA // EF
19. **AB // DC**
20. **AB, CD, GH, ML**
21. **AB, LM, HG, FE, ON, KJ**

22.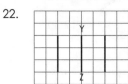

23.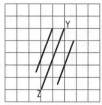

24.

Unit 18: Area and Perimeter

1. **7**
2. **10**
3. **6**
4. **12**
5. **5**
6. (a) **13**   (e) **10**
   (b) **9**   (f) **B, C**
   (c) **9**   (g) **D**
   (d) **8**   (h) **A**
7. **14**
8. **18**
9. **22**
10. **20**
11. **28**
12. (a) **11**   (g) **18**
    (b) **14**   (h) **20**
    (c) **12**   (i) **D**
    (d) **16**   (j) **A**
    (e) **20**   (k) **C**
    (f) **22**   (l) **B**
13. 9 + 4 + 3 + 5 + 6 + 9 = **36** cm
14. 13 + 10 + 15 + 9 = **47** cm
15. 11 + 14 + 17 = **42** in.
16. 15 + 9 + 9 + 15 + 22 = **70** m
17. 30 + 2 + 7 + 6 + 8 + 5 + 15 + 14 = **87** m
18. 8 × 7 = **56** in.²
    8 + 7 + 8 + 7 = **30** in.

Singapore Math Level 3A & 3B

19. $3 \times 12 = $ **36** cm²
    $3 + 12 + 3 + 12 = $ **30** cm
20. $13 \times 4 = $ **52** ft.²
    $13 + 4 + 13 + 4 = $ **34** ft.
21. $6 \times 6 = $ **36** cm²
    $6 + 6 + 6 + 6 = $ **24** cm
22. $15 \times 8 = $ **120** cm²
    $15 + 8 + 15 + 8 = $ **46** cm
23.

8 cm
4 cm | | 4 cm
8 cm

    $4 + 8 + 4 + 8 = 24$ cm
    Andrew needs **24 cm** of wire.
24.

8 cm
6 cm

    $6 \times 8 = 48$ m²
    Mercy sweeps **48 m²** of floor space.
25. $240 \div 4 = 60$ yd.
    The length of each side of the square field is **60 yd.**

Review 7

1.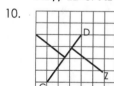

2. (a) **16**
   (b) **22**
3. **9, 2**
4. **AH $\perp$ HG, GF $\perp$ HG,**
   GF $\perp$ FE
5. (a) **z**   (c) **y**
   (b) **y**   (d) **z, x, w, y**
6. (a) **20**   (f) **16**
   (b) **10**   (g) **18**
   (c) **14**   (h) **24**
   (d) **11**   (i) **B**
   (e) **18**   (j) **D**
7. **AB // CD, HG // ML**
8. $24 + 14 + 6 + 9 + 18 + 5 = $ **76 in.**
9. **BA // KL** or **DC // HJ** or
   AL // BC or **AL // JK** or
   BC // ED or **JK // HG** or
   AL // ED or **AL // HG**
10.

11.

12. $32 \times 8 = $ **256** in.²
    $32 + 8 + 32 + 8 = $ **80** in.
13. $12 \times 12 = $ **144 cm²**
14. $9 + 9 + 9 + 9 + 9 + 9 + 9 + 9 = 72$ cm
    The perimeter of the figure is **72 cm.**

15. $15 \times 2 = 30$ in.
    Its length is 30 in.
    $15 + 30 + 15 + 30 = 90$ in.
    The perimeter of the box is **90 cm.**
16. $20 \times 8 = 160$ in.²
    The area of the room is **160 m².**
17. $30 \times 15 = 450$ in.²
    $450 - 80 = 370$ in.²
    The area of the remaining wrapping paper was **370 in.²**
18. $14 \times 11 = 154$ cm²
    $154 \times 2 = 308$ cm²
    The area of the piece of drawing paper was **308 cm².**
19. $25 - 13 = 12$ cm
    $13 + 9 + 12 + 7 + 25 + 16 = 82$ cm
    The perimeter of the remaining cardboard is **82 cm.**
20. $5 + 8 + 5 + 8 + 5 + 8 + 5 + 8 = 52$ cm
    The perimeter of the two stickers is **52 cm.**

Final Review

1. (a) **AB $\perp$ GH, CD $\perp$ GH**
   (b) **AB//CD**
2. **5:30 P.M.**

   15 min.   30 min.
   4:45 P.M.   5:00 P.M.   5:30 P.M.

3. (a) 300 cm $+ 7$ cm $= $ **3** m **7** cm
   (b) $43,000$ g $+ 210$ g $= $ **43,210** g
   (c) $80,000$ mL $+ 10$ mL $= $ **80,010** mL
   (d) $4,000$ m $+ 40$ m $= $ **4,040** m
4. (a) **books**
   (b) **40**
   (c) $55 - 15 = $ **40**
   (d) $20 - 5 = $ **15**
   (e) $15 + 5 = $ **20**
5. (a) **$3.30**
       $\$2.35 + \$0.95 = \$3.30$
   (b) **$1.40**
       $\$2.00 + \$1.60 = \$3.60$
       $\$5.00 - \$3.60 = \$1.40$
   (c) **$0.30 / 30¢**
       $\$0.95 + \$1.35 = \$2.30$
       $\$2.30 - \$2 = \$0.30$
   (d) **notebook, pen, and sharpener**
       $\$1.60 + \$1.35 + \$0.95 = \$3.90$
6. (a) $\dfrac{3 \times 3}{7 \times 3} = \dfrac{9}{\mathbf{21}}$
   (b) $\dfrac{2 \times 4}{4 \times 4} = \dfrac{\mathbf{8}}{16}$
   (c) $\dfrac{8 \times 4}{11 \times 4} = \dfrac{32}{\mathbf{44}}$
   (d) $\dfrac{4 \times 3}{9 \times 3} = \dfrac{\mathbf{12}}{27}$
7. (a) $\dfrac{8 \div 4}{12 \div 4} = \dfrac{\mathbf{2}}{\mathbf{3}}$
   (b) $\dfrac{3 \div 3}{6 \div 3} = \dfrac{\mathbf{1}}{\mathbf{2}}$
   (c) $\dfrac{6 \div 2}{8 \div 2} = \dfrac{\mathbf{3}}{\mathbf{4}}$

Singapore Math Level 3A & 3B

(d) $\dfrac{4 \div 2}{10 \div 2} = \dfrac{2}{5}$

8. **39**

9.

10. $\dfrac{1}{4}, \dfrac{3}{8}, \dfrac{3}{4}$

$\dfrac{1 \times 3}{4 \times 3} = \dfrac{3}{12}$

11. (a) **4,035**

    4 km 35 m = 4,000 m + 35 m
    = 4,035 m

    (b) **2,257**

    1 km 210 m + 1 km 47 m = 2 km 257 m
    = 2,000 m + 257 m
    = 2,257 m

    (c) 4 km 35 m + 3 km 939 m = **7 km 974 m**

    (d) **by the school**

    (e) 7 km 974 m – 2 km 257 m = **5 km 717 m**

12. **558.35**

    $360.50 + $197.85 = $558.35

13. **7, 59**

    1,036 cm – 277 cm = 759 cm = 7 m 59 cm

14. **16, 316**

    7,004 m + 9,312 m = 16,316 m = 16 km 316 m

15. **381.30**

    $469.20 – $87.90 = $381.30

16. **20, 441**

    63,097 mL – 42,656 mL = 20,441 mL = 20 L 441 mL

17. **73, 995**

    44,300 g + 29,695 g = 73,995 g = 73 kg 995 g

18. (a) **g**
    (b) **kg**

19. **1:55 P.M.**

20. $\dfrac{1}{9} + \dfrac{2 \times 3}{3 \times 3} = \dfrac{1}{9} + \dfrac{6}{9} = \dfrac{7}{9}$

21. 12 × 10 = 120 m²

    Robert will pour **120 ft.²** of concrete.

22.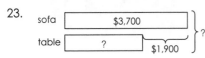

    125,600 – 60,700 = 64,900
    64,900 = 64 kg 900 g
    The lion has a mass of 64 kg 900 g.
    125,600 + 64,900 = 190,500
    190,500 g = 190 kg 500 g
    The total mass of the two animals is **190 kg 500 g**.

23.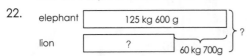

    $3,700 – $1,900 = $1,800
    The table cost $1,800.
    $3,700 + $1,800 = $5,500
    Marley paid **$5,500** for the furniture in all.

24.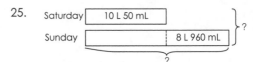

    93,650 + 6,770 = 100,420
    100,420 m = 100 km 420 m
    The ship travels **100 km 420 m** altogether.

25.

    10,050 + 8,960 = 19,010
    19,010 mL = 19 L 10 mL
    Mary cooked 19 L 10 mL of chicken soup on Sunday.
    10,050 + 19,010 = 29,060
    29,060 mL = 29 L 60 mL
    The total volume of chicken soup that she cooked on both days was **29 L 60 mL**.

Challenge Questions

1. Use 'Guess and Check' method.
   (2 × $10) + (1 × $5) + (4 × $1) + (2 × 25¢) + (2 × 10¢)
   = $29.70
   The bills and coins she gave the cashier were **two ten-dollar bills**, **one five-dollar bill**, **four one-dollar bills**, **two quarters**, and **two dimes**.

2.

	1 km		1 km	
Jamie's house		garden		school

   2 × 1 = 2 km
   The distance from Jamie's house to her school is **2 km**.

3. Use 'Guess and Check' method.
   12 + 34 = 46
   43 + 21 = 64
   A = **1**, B = **2**, C = **3**, D = **4**

4. 1 m + 50 cm = 1 m 50 cm
   Plant B is 1 m 50 cm tall.
   1 m – 5 cm = 100 cm – 5 cm = 95 cm
   Plant C is 95 cm tall.
   Plant B is the tallest and Plant C is the shortest.
   1 m 50 cm + 95 cm = 2 m 45 cm
   The total height of the tallest and the shortest plants is **2 m 45 cm**.

5.

   Tokyo: 7 A.M.
   Singapore: 6 P.M.

   The time of his flight in Singapore was **11 P.M.** on **September 13**.

6. $\dfrac{1 \times 2}{4 \times 2} = \dfrac{2}{8}$

254

$\frac{2}{8}$ of the string was immersed in oil and water.

$\frac{1}{8} \rightarrow 5$ cm

$\frac{2}{8} \rightarrow 5 \times 2 = 10$ cm

$\frac{8}{8} \rightarrow 5 \times 8 = 40$ cm

The total length of the string was **40 cm**.

7.
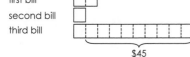
first bill

second bill

third bill

$45

9 units $\rightarrow$ $45

1 unit $\rightarrow$ $45 ÷ 9 = $5

13 units $\rightarrow$ $5 × 13 = $65

Ken has **$65**.

8.
| 12 hours earlier |
12:00 P.M.	12:00 A.M.
Christmas Eve	Christmas Day
(New York)	(Singapore)

The time in New York will be **12:00 P.M.** on **Christmas Eve**.

9.
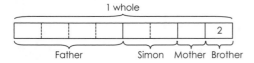
1 whole

Father   Simon Mother Brother

$8 \times 2 = 16$

There were **16** pieces of pizza at first.

10. There are 3 bills. One is 5 times the amount of each of the other 2.

$5 $1 [   ]

$1 [   ]

$1 [   ]

$5 × $1 = $5

$5 + $1 + $1 = $7

The change was $7.

$25 − $7 = $18

The groceries were **$18**.

11. $30 ÷ 3 = 10$

$10 × 1$ in. $= 10$ in.

The bean plant will grow **10 in.** after 30 days.

12. From the given numbers,

$118 + 159 = 277$

$387 + 513 = 900$

$118 + 269 = 387$

$277 + 623 = 900$

$623 − 269 = 354$ or $513 − 159 = 354$

The missing number is **354**.

Notes